The Minister's Life of Obedience

Dr. Phillip Gary Richards

The Minister's Life of Obedience
by Dr. Phillip Gary Richards

Printed in the United States of America

ISBN 1-59781-054-1

Unless otherwise indicated, all scriptural quotations are from the *King James Version* of the Bible. Additional scripture references are from: *New American Standard Bible*, Nashville, TN, by Thomas Nelson Publishers; *Young's Literal Translation*, Grand Rapids, MI, by Guardian Press; the *Amplified Bible*, Expanded Edition, Grand Rapids, MI, Copyright © 1965 by Zondervan Publishing House; and the *New Revised Standard Version*, Nashville, TN, Copyright © 1989 by Thomas Nelson Publishers.

www.xulonpress.com

FOREWORD

By Dr. Douglas J. Wingate

President and Founder of Life Christian University

In the pages of this book Dr. Phillip Richards unfolds some of the most essential truths for a victorious Christian life and for success in the ministry. The book contains vital information on fundamentals for personal spiritual growth and exposes the wiles of the devil, designed to destroy one's life and ministry.

As an experienced educator and mentor of ministers, I confirm that the forming of solid morals and ethical Christian character is the cornerstone of ministerial life and the only guarantee of success in fulfilling one's divine call and destiny. Sadly far too few books are written for the purpose of character development that really exalt the high standards of excellence demanded by God's Word. Since the Holy Spirit can only consistently anoint a person who has been transformed, having a mind renewed by God's precepts and power, *The Minister's Life of Obedience* is a "must read" for every sincere minister and ministry student. Dr. Richards rightly divides a multitude of scriptures that will leave the reader with increased faith and the ability to humbly obey the guidance of our great Shepherd, the Lord Jesus.

Only someone who lives and walks in the truths revealed in this book qualifies to deliver them to others. I can testify that Dr. Richards is that qualified man. He has been a close friend to my wife and me for many years. My children call him Uncle Phil. Over the years he has been a guest many times in our home. I have had the opportunity to observe him as he stood the tests of time and adversity and continually maintained a victorious life and ministry. As a seasoned pastor, evangelist, psalmist and missionary, his gifts and experience are invaluable to the training of today's ministers of the end-time harvest. His teaching ministry is a great blessing to all the students at the Life Christian University extension campus in Buckhannon, West Virginia, where he is a professor.

Enjoy this book as you read it. Take the time to meditate on the truths contained within so that the Lord can speak to you, minister to you and help you be better equipped to run your race and fulfill your divine destiny.

Dr. Douglas J. Wingate
President and Founder of Life Christian University

TABLE OF CONTENTS

INTRODUCTION

" A lso I heard the voice of the Lord, saying, whom shall I send, and who will go for us? Then said I, Here am I; send me" (Is. 6:8, KJV). The Lord is still asking this same question today. "Whom shall I send, and who will go for us?" The answer of Isaiah is the focus of this book: "Here am I; send me." For before there can be a response to God's call, there must be the decision in the heart of the one answering the call to obey. Obedience to God's call to the ministry is just the beginning of a life of obedience. Indeed before one can be a minister, one must be an obedient minister. Therefore, this book is not about the life of the minister only. It is not a philosophical discussion of some religious idea about the minister. But rather as you read on you will discover this book addresses the biblical picture of the minister's life—a life of obedience to the Lord and His Word.

Obedience to the Lord must be a daily affair beginning with obedience to the call and completed obedience to the will of the Lord on the earth. From the beginning of the call to the ending of the call, obedience must be a way of life. Obedience to the Lord starts with a decision and continues by making the right decisions every day. And that is the very heart of what the Lord really wants out of all of us, to daily decide to obey Him, not only in part of our lives, but in every aspect of our lives.

Therefore, even if you have not been called to stand in one or more of the five-fold ministry gifts, this book is still for you. For all of us in the body of Christ desire to hear the Lord say one day, "Well done." It is therefore my deepest wish that as you read this book you will be inspired, challenged and determined to obey the Lord in every area of your life. If you are a minister, remember that your ministry must be a life of obedience.

I.

CALLED AND SEPARATED TO THE MINISTRY

"And no man taketh this honor unto himself, but he that is called of God, as was Aaron. So also Christ glorified not himself to be made an high priest; but he that said unto him, Thou art my Son, to day have I begotten thee" (Heb. 5:4-5, KJV). The ministry is not a chosen profession. It is not something one does because one thinks the ministry would be a good career. It is not a profession ordained by man. The ministry is first and foremost a call. This call comes from the Father God Himself. There is not a higher authority. There is no higher honor. There is no greater privilege. All who would desire the work of the ministry must understand that the minister's life of obedience begins with this call. Even our Lord and Savior Jesus Christ began His earthly and present-day ministry with the call of God. Notice our text says "no man takes this honor to himself."

Men and women have been hearing and answering that call for thousands of years. These men and women have come from all walks of life and ages and backgrounds. Such diversities of people and character, with different personalities and talents and abilities, have answered that call. And while all who have been called share many things from God that make up the ministry, such as the anointing to do God's will, yet all are different. The plan of the Lord for one person is one of a kind. It is based on a "one on one" relationship.

Hidden deep within the heart of the Father is that call. It is hidden in His heart alone until the time appointed of the Father God to reveal that call to the one called. The call is "from the foundation of the world" (Eph. 1:4, KJV). But the revelation of that call comes in "the time appointed of the Father" (Gal. 4:2, KJV). God's Word gives us a wonderful example of this call of God upon the life of the minister in the life of the apostle Paul.

As you read the following example in God's Word you will notice several things about that call of God.

And Saul, yet breathing out threatenings and slaughter against the disciples of the Lord, went unto the high priest, and desired of him letters to Damascus to the synagogues, that if he found any of this way, whether they were men or women, he might bring them bound unto Jerusalem. And as he journeyed, he came near Damascus: and suddenly there shined round about him a light from heaven: and he fell to the earth, and heard a voice saying unto him, Saul, Saul, why persecutest thou me? And he said, Who art thou, Lord? And the Lord said, I am Jesus whom thou persecutest: it is hard for thee to kick against the pricks. And he trembling and astonished said, Lord, what wilt thou have me to do? And the Lord said unto him, Arise, and go into the city, and it shall be told thee what thou must do (Acts 9:1-6).

Notice that even though Paul thought he was doing God's will, he was doing just the opposite. He was actually persecuting the church of God. While Paul was educated in the Jewish religion he was far from what God wanted him to do. Notice what he said about himself in Galatians.

For ye have heard of my conversation in time past in the Jews' religion, how that beyond measure I persecuted the church of God, and wasted it: and profited in the Jews' religion above many my equals in mine own nation, being more exceedingly zealous of the traditions of my fathers (Gal. 1:13-14).

But Paul finally asked the question he should have asked long before the Lord appeared to him on the road to Damascus. Notice in the above text he said, "Lord, what wilt thou have me to do?" The Lord told Paul to "go into the city and it shall be told thee what thou must do."

Let's continue to look at what else the Word of God has to say about Paul's call to the ministry.

And the men which journeyed with him stood speechless, hearing a voice, but seeing no man. And Saul arose from the earth; and when his eyes were opened, he saw no man: but they led him by the hand, and brought him into Damascus. And he was three days without sight, and neither did eat nor drink. And there was a certain disciple at Damascus, named Ananias; and to him said the Lord in a vision, Ananias. And he said, Behold, I am here, Lord. And the Lord said unto him, Arise, and go into the street which is called Straight, and inquire in the house of Judas for one called Saul, of Tarsus: for, behold, he prayeth, and hath seen

in a vision a man named Ananias coming in, and putting his hand on him, that he might receive his sight. Then Ananias answered, Lord, I have heard by many of this man, how much evil he hath done to thy saints at Jerusalem: and here he hath authority from the chief priests to bind all that call on thy name. But the Lord said unto him, Go thy way: for he is a chosen vessel unto me, to bear my name before the Gentiles, and kings, and the children of Israel: for I will show him how great things he must suffer for my name's sake (Acts 9:7-16).

Notice that the Lord said Paul was a "chosen vessel." When was Paul chosen? According to God's Word it was before the foundation of the world. "According as he hath chosen us in him before the foundation of the world" (Eph. 1:4, KJV). Not all of us who are called into the ministry have or will have such an experience as Paul did when he received his call. But all of us can rest assured that if we are called to the ministry we will surely know it.

Now I want you to see that when Paul realized it was the Lord who was speaking to him and telling him to go into the city to hear more later from God, he had a choice to make. He had to choose to *obey* what the Lord said to him. And not only obey then, but also to continue to obey all that the Lord wanted him to do the rest of his life. After receiving the *call* to the ministry, then there must be the *separating* to the ministry.

Both the call and the separation come from the Lord. From the time one receives the call to the ministry and the time the Lord chooses to separate one into the ministry will always be a period of preparation *"for"* the ministry that is greatly determined by one's obedience to the Lord in all things. Paul learned this truth well. When he wrote to the Romans he started off his letter by saying, "Paul, a servant of Jesus Christ, called to be an apostle, separated unto the gospel of God" (Rom. 1:1, KJV).

Many young ministers have never understood this principle and therefore have launched out into the ministry all too soon, even though they had the call of God upon their lives. Again let us look at the Word of God concerning Paul's ministry to see this illustrated.

Now there were in the church that was at Antioch certain prophets and teachers; as Barnabas, and Simeon that was called Niger, and Lucius of Cyrene, and Manaen, which had been brought up with Herod the tetrarch, and Saul. As they ministered to the Lord, and fasted, the Holy Ghost said, Separate me Barnabas and Saul for the work whereunto I have called them. And when they had fasted and prayed, and laid their hands on them, they sent them away. So they, being sent forth by the Holy Ghost, departed unto Seleucia; and from thence they sailed to Cyprus (Acts 13:1-3).

It was the Lord by the power of the Holy Spirit who separated Paul to do the work he was called to do. As I have already said, a call to the ministry is a call to preparation first. I know in my own life that the call of God was always there. Even when I was very young I sensed that call. I didn't understand it, but I could tell God's hand was upon my life. Even before I was born again I could tell the Lord was with me. Over and over again He spared my life when the devil tried to take it. I'm sure you also could agree that the hand of the Lord was your deliverance when the devil tried to take your life.

After I received Christ into my heart as my personal savior I was aware even more that the Lord had a work for me to do. I still did not understand it, but as the years progressed that call drew me into the presence of the Lord more often. All believers will be led into the presence of the Lord; but those who are called to the ministry will sense that drawing even to a greater degree. It is more real because the Lord has that timing for each one to come to the reality as Paul did that they are called into the full-time ministry.

I remember when I was in high school and it was time to graduate; like all high school graduates I tried to decide what I wanted to do with my life. I knew I wanted to do something for the Lord, but I didn't know what to do. I remember talking to my father about whether or not I should go to college, and I will never forget what he told me. He said it was always God's will for one to better oneself. So I took his advice and went to Lee College in Cleveland, Tennessee.

Having always loved music and sensing that call upon me that I didn't fully understand, I majored in church music and decided I was going to become a minister of music. After only a year and a half, though, I moved back to West Virginia. I started to work with my father in construction and thought I was doing fine when I found myself sick and asking the Lord to heal me. After three days, while walking to my bedroom, the power of God touched me and healed me instantly. I remember falling to my face to thank the Lord for my healing and hearing His voice in my spirit, saying, "Son, I've called you to work for me, not the world." I told the Lord, yes, I would obey Him and immediately set out to do just that.

Believing I was called only to the music ministry, I inquired in my denomination about all possible openings for a minister of music. One door opened for me in Mansfield, Ohio, where I took a job as associate pastor and music minister.

It was there I first heard the Word-of-Faith message. And it was there I heard the Lord speak to me again in a prayer room at the church and say, "My son, I'm calling you to *preach* My Word." What he said to me was such a revelation, as I never thought of myself as a preacher. But God knew what He was doing, and I trusted Him.

That was in 1975. So I immediately started preaching the best I could. But in 1977 I was led to enroll in Rhema Bible Training Center in Broken Arrow, Oklahoma, where I eventually graduated. You see I was now *called* to the ministry but not yet *separated* to the ministry. But the day finally came in 1986 when Kenneth E. Hagin laid his hands on me and ordained me into the full-time ministry. And what a difference it made in my life after being separated by the Lord. Now I want you to observe what the apostle Paul continued to say about himself.

"But when it pleased God, who separated me from my mother's womb, and called me by his grace, to reveal his Son in me, that I might preach him among the heathen; immediately I conferred not with flesh and blood" (Gal. 1:15, KJV). As far as God was concerned, Paul was separated from his mother's womb. But as far as Paul was concerned, he had to receive the revelation of not only the call of God upon his life, but also the need to be separated by the Lord.

It is interesting to note that the Greek word translated "separated" in this verse is *aphorizo* and means "to set off by boundary, to limit, exclude, appoint, etc.:—divide, separate, sever" (Strong's Hebrew Greek Dictionary). In other words the Lord is saying He has a boundary for the life of the one He is calling to the ministry. There is a "setting apart" to work for Him. Our challenge is to stay within that boundary.

All that concerns the minister's life must revolve around the Lord's plan in all aspects of life. Indeed God's Word has much to say about this separation. Notice the following scripture.

But in a great house there are not only vessels of gold and of silver, but also of wood and of earth; and some to honor, and some to dishonor. If a man therefore purge himself from these, he shall be a vessel unto honor, sanctified, and meet for the

master's use, and prepared unto every good work (2 Tim. 2:20-21).

Here we can observe that all of us have much to do with the call of God upon us. The one called to the ministry must "purge himself" from all that will hinder that call from being fulfilled. Is it easy? No, it is not. Is it necessary? Yes, it is absolutely necessary before the blessings of the Lord can flow upon the life of that individual to the point where they can be used of God. In the Old Testament we can find another example of how the minister must be obedient to the call and the separation of the Lord. In 1 Kings 19 we find the story of Elijah and Elisha. In the previous chapter we read of the story of Elijah calling down fire from heaven to consume the sacrifice and by the power of God slaying more than 450 false prophets of Baal.

As you know, afterward he ran from Jezebel and felt sorry for himself. The Lord began dealing with him there; eventually, because of his complaining, the Lord told him to go anoint Elisha to be prophet in his place. Let's look at Scripture now to learn more about obedience to the call and the separation.

And Jehu the son of Nimshi shalt thou anoint to be king over Israel: and Elisha the son of Shaphat of Abelmeholah shalt thou anoint to be prophet in thy room. And it shall come to pass, that him that escapeth the sword of Hazael shall Jehu slay: and him that escapeth from the sword of Jehu shall Elisha slay.

Yet I have left me seven thousand in Israel, all the knees which have not bowed unto Baal, and every mouth which hath not kissed him. So he departed thence, and found Elisha the son of Shaphat, who

was plowing with twelve yoke of oxen before him, and he with the twelfth: and Elijah passed by him, and cast his mantle upon him. And he left the oxen, and ran after Elijah, and said, Let me, I pray thee, kiss my father and my mother, and then I will follow thee. And he said unto him, Go back again: for what have I done to thee? And he returned back from him, and took a yoke of oxen, and slew them, and boiled their flesh with the instruments of the oxen, and gave unto the people, and they did eat. Then he arose, and went after Elijah, and ministered unto him (1 Kings 19:16-21).

We can learn numerous things from this passage. First, notice that Elisha understood immediately what was happening when Elijah cast his mantle upon him. Elisha knew the mantle was a type of the anointing of the Lord. He may not have known much about it, but he knew God was *calling* him and that he had to be obedient to that call. He learned that he had to put that call first. When he wanted to go kiss his father and mother the prophet Elijah told him to "go back again; for what have I done to thee?"

In other words, if Elisha was going to put other things first, then he could forget about the call of God upon him. Elisha understood what Elijah meant and immediately killed his oxen and followed Elijah and ministered to him. So Elisha began his ministry properly by being obedient to God's call upon his life. Again the mantle represented the anointing of God, or the equipping of God to enable him to be a minister.

Though the call was upon him and he knew it, he was not yet *separated* to the ministry. His obedience had to continue throughout his time of *preparation*. As he ministered to Elijah he was in preparation. As we minister to others we likewise are in preparation.

We will continue to learn much about obedience to the call and obedience in the separation of the life of Elisha as we resume reading God's Word. Notice in 2 Kings 2 we have the recording of the beginning of his separation into the ministry.

And it came to pass, when the Lord would take up Elijah into heaven by a whirlwind, that Elijah went with Elisha from Gilgal. And Elijah said unto Elisha, Tarry here, I pray thee; for the Lord hath sent me to Bethel. And Elisha said unto him, As the Lord liveth, and as thy soul liveth, I will not leave thee. So they went down to Bethel. And the sons of the prophets that were at Bethel came forth to Elisha, and said unto him, Knowest thou that the Lord will take away thy master from thy head to day? And he said, Yea, I know it; hold ye your peace.

And Elijah said unto him, Elisha, tarry here, I pray thee; for the Lord hath sent me to Jericho. And he said, As the Lord liveth, and as thy soul liveth, I will not leave thee. So they came to Jericho. And the sons of the prophets that were at Jericho came to Elisha, and said unto him, Knowest thou that the Lord will take away thy master from thy head to day? And he answered, Yea, I know it; hold ye your peace. And Elijah said unto him, Tarry, I pray thee, here; for the Lord hath sent me to Jordan. And he said, As the Lord liveth, and as thy soul liveth, I will not leave thee. And they two went on. And fifty men of the sons of the prophets went, and stood to view afar off: and they two stood by Jordan. And Elijah took his mantle, and wrapped it together, and smote the waters, and

they were divided hither and thither, so that they two went over on dry ground.

And it came to pass, when they were gone over, that Elijah said unto Elisha, Ask what I shall do for thee, before I be taken away from thee. And Elisha said, I pray thee, let a double portion of thy spirit be upon me. And he said, Thou hast asked a hard thing: nevertheless, if thou see me when I am taken from thee, it shall be so unto thee; but if not, it shall not be. And it came to pass, as they still went on, and talked, that, behold, there appeared a chariot of fire, and horses of fire, and parted them both asunder; and Elijah went up by a whirlwind into heaven.

And Elisha saw it, and he cried, My father, my father, the chariot of Israel, and the horsemen thereof. And he saw him no more: and he took hold of his own clothes, and rent them in two pieces. He took up also the mantle of Elijah that fell from him, and went back, and stood by the bank of Jordan; And he took the mantle of Elijah that fell from him, and smote the waters, and said, Where is the Lord God of Elijah? and when he also had smitten the waters, they parted hither and thither: and Elisha went over (2 Kings 2:1-14).

Elisha had every opportunity to become discouraged as he was following Elijah that last day. He could have listened to Elijah and stayed in each of the cities in which Elijah wanted him to remain. But he stayed right with Elijah because he knew he wanted to be in the ministry more than anything else in the world. He was obedient to the call of preparation.

Oh, how easy it would have been to listen to the sons of the prophets as they also tried to discourage Elisha from going on with Elijah. But he pressed in. He persevered. He would not allow anything to stop him from obeying God. And that is exactly how one must press on into the call of God upon one's life.

It is never easy. For the enemy of our souls would do everything within his ability to stop us from obeying the call of God upon our lives. At any moment we could say no. At any moment we could say not now. At any moment we could allow ourselves to be sidetracked. Often hindrances come with those things we must do in life. But we cannot afford to put those things first.

At every step along life's pathway we will be making the choice to obey the Lord or disobey; to run the race the Lord has called us to run or lag back and put other things first. The choice is ours. The Lord will never force us to do His will. Yet He understands we will have obstacles, so He is also there in the test to put us over.

We can rest assured that if we will do our part, the Lord will always do His part. He will provide the strength, the courage, the motivation to do what we could never do in ourselves. When Elisha passed the test of obedience, he became ready for the separation into the ministry that the Lord had for him all along. And so it is with us as well. We must also pass this same test. As ministers we must understand this fact; for if we pass this test of obedience to the call of God upon our lives we also will become ready for the plan the Lord had for us all along. Remember what the apostle Paul had to say about depending on the Lord in order to fulfill the call of God upon his life?

"But by the grace of God I am what I am: and his grace which was bestowed upon me was not in vain; but I labored more abundantly than they all: yet not I, but the grace of God which was with me" (1 Cor. 15:10, KJV). Notice Paul said it was by the *grace* of God that made Paul what he was. Paul learned to depend upon that grace. He understood that if he did his part by being obedient the Lord would do His part by enabling Paul to follow God's will.

Again using myself as an example, I remember my first class at Rhema Bible Training Center. It was Old Testament Prophets, taught by Rev. Cooper Beaty. He informed us we would be graded on three things. One third of our grade would come from one test. One third of our grade would come from writing a research paper. And one third of our grade would come from our notes.

Well, it had been several years since I had been in college, so I had more than a little trouble in taking good notes. And Rev. Beaty taught so fast that all the students knew him as Machine-Gun Beaty. I believe he retains that title to this day.

Needless to say I thought I would fail. I remember walking down that crowded hall after class and asking the Lord in my heart, "Lord, did you send me here to fail?" Within my spirit I clearly heard the Lord say, "Son, if you will do your part, I will do Mine." I knew instantly what the Lord meant. In other words if I would apply myself, He would help me. That is exactly what Paul meant when he talked about the grace of God. He said, "I labored more than they, yet not I but God's grace in me" (1 Cor. 15:10).

As human beings all of us have our fleshly side with which we must contend. And here is where faith comes in. You see, obedience is faith in action. The apostle James said, "But wilt thou know, O vain man, that faith without works is dead?" (James 2:20, KJV). Of course we know the word *works* here means corresponding actions. In other words we can have all the faith in the world, but without actions our faith is dead.

James went on to say: "Was not Abraham our father justified by works, when he had offered Isaac his son upon the altar? Seest thou how faith wrought with his works and by works was faith made perfect?" (James 2:21-22, KJV). Our Lord Jesus Christ fully understood these principles. He knew He also had to respond to the call of God upon His life. He also knew He had to be separated as well.

Obedience was something our Lord Himself had to learn. We find Him being the perfect example of obedience to the will of the Father His entire life. But He did so the same way we do, and that is by the anointing and the power of God.

"Though he were a Son, yet learned he obedience by the things which he suffered; and being made perfect, he became the author of eternal salvation unto all them that obey him" (Heb. 5:8-9, KJV). Notice that Jesus learned obedience by the things He suffered, and so must we.

Remember that our Lord said of Himself, "Believest thou not that I am in the Father, and the Father in me? The words that I speak unto you I speak not of myself: but the Father that dwelleth in me, he doeth the works" (John 14:10, KJV).

"Then answered Jesus and said unto them, Verily, verily, I say unto you, The Son can do nothing of himself, but what he seeth the Father do: for what things soever he doeth, these also doeth the Son likewise" (John 5:19, KJV). In other words, though Jesus was the Son of God, yet He had to become submissive and obedient to the will of God to the extent that He did nothing on His own.

Here is one of the greatest mysteries in the Word of God. That Jesus the Son of God could do nothing by Himself. He had to depend upon the anointing just as we do to do the works of God. Remember that Jesus was baptized in the River Jordan by John the Baptist and was filled with the Holy Spirit. But immediately He was led into the wilderness to be tempted of the devil. Let's look at the Word of God further concerning the ministry of Jesus.

And Jesus, when he was baptized, went up straightway out of the water: and, lo, the heavens

were opened unto him, and he saw the Spirit of God descending like a dove, and lighting upon him: and, lo, a voice from heaven, saying, This is my beloved Son, in whom I am well pleased. Then was Jesus led up of the Spirit into the wilderness to be tempted of the devil (Matt. 3:16-17; 4:1).

Notice in answer to the call Jesus was baptized and filled with the Spirit. But in *separation* to the call of God He was led into the wilderness to be tempted of the devil. This is what Hebrews means when it says He learned obedience. For forty days Jesus was tested. And after having passed the test the Word says, "And Jesus returned in the power of the Spirit into Galilee: and there went out a fame of him through the entire region round about. And he taught in their synagogues, being glorified of all" (Luke 4:14-15, KJV).

So our Lord fully understood what it meant to be called and what it meant to be separated into the work of the Lord. Since He is our example, I'm so glad He was faithful. I'm so glad He obeyed all the way, even until death. "Jesus saith unto them, my meat is to do the will of him that sent me, and to finish his work" (John 4:34, KJV). Let's purpose in our hearts to follow the example our Lord Jesus Christ has set for us and say with Him, "Our meat is to do the will of Him that sends us."

For those of us who are called into the full-time ministry ours is a daily challenge. It is a challenge to stay sanctified so the Lord can continue to separate us into other aspects of ministry. We must never forget that the call is the Lord's and the separation is also the Lord's. Richard Baxter, an Episcopal pastor during the years 1615-1691, once said,

Self-interest is a bad trade to choose. Thus self-denial is absolutely necessary for every Christian. But it is doubly necessary for a minister of the

gospel, because he has to have a double dedication and sanctification to God. Without self-denial he cannot serve God even for one hour (13).

Truer words have never been spoken. I also believe that without this knowledge before us we will be tempted to get ahead of God and His plans for us. Our temptation much of the time lies in the unwillingness to pay the price of the ministry. Our Lord set the right example. He paid the price of self-denial when He went into the wilderness to be tempted by the devil.

By avoiding the time of testings often we are only keeping ourselves from taking the next step God the Father has planned for our destiny. But by yielding to His purpose in preparing us we are then in a position to be separated by the Lord into the fullness of His will. And that is the place we are called to, not just once but every day of our lives.

II.

QUALIFIED BY THE LORD

As the minister lives the life of obedience it must not be forgotten that because the calling comes from the Lord, the qualifications come also from the Lord. Without reminding ourselves of this truth we will find ourselves trying to do the work of the Lord in our own strength. Such labor will only frustrate us as well as hinder the will of our Father God from being accomplished both in our lives and in the ministries to which we are called.

I haven't met the first person yet who doesn't have something to overcome in this area. Failing to remember the Lord qualifies us will either bring condemnation and self-pity or worldly pride. Either way, both are not only wrong but will grieve the Holy Spirit and block the blessing of the Lord from flowing into our lives. The enemy would like nothing more than to get us as ministers looking on ourselves, our strength, our wisdom, our ability, and not on the Lord from whom comes our help.

Remembering the Lord qualifies us has much to do with our life of obedience. It is a truth that must at all times remain before us. When we start our day the Lord qualifies us. When we prepare for ministry the Lord qualifies us. As we minister to others the Lord qualifies us. In our darkest hour the Lord qualifies us. Wherever or whatever the Lord asks us to do we must remember it is He who has qualified us to do the work of the ministry.

Let's notice the Word of God again to find out what it tells us about being qualified to the work of the ministry: "For the gifts and calling of God are without repentance" (Rom. 11:29). Here we learn that the calling of God is without repentance, meaning that the Lord will never withdraw His calling.

But we also learn that the *gifts* also are without repentance. Again that means God the Father will qualify each person called to the ministry with gifts He will not revoke. Both the *call* comes from the Lord and the *gifts* come from the Lord. Paul said in his letter to the Corinthians:

Not that we are sufficient of ourselves to think any thing as of ourselves; but our sufficiency is of God; who also hath made us able ministers of the new testament; not of the letter, but of the spirit: for the letter killeth, but the spirit giveth life (2 Cor. 3:5-6).

Notice Paul said that God has made us able ministers. The Greek word translated "able" is *hidanoo*, which means to "qualify" (Strong's Hebrew Greek Dictionary). Praise God we are able ministers. We are able because He has qualified us Himself to do what He has called us to do. The Amplified Bible reads:

Not that we are fit (qualified and sufficient in ability) of ourselves to form personal judgments or to claim or count anything as coming from

us, but our power and ability and sufficiency are from God. It is He who has qualified us (making us to be fit and worthy and sufficient) as ministers and dispensers of a new covenant of salvation through Christ, not ministers of the letter (of legally written code) but of the Spirit; for the code (of the Law) kills, but the Holy Spirit makes alive (2 Cor. 3:5-6, Amp).

So we are fit, made able, qualified and sufficient in ability by almighty God Himself. All the power of heaven backs us up, as we become obedient to the call of God upon our lives. The Word of God is full of examples that teach us this truth both explicitly and implicitly. Indeed the example used earlier of Elijah and Elisha illustrates so clearly what the apostle Paul has said about being qualified by the Lord.

When Elijah placed his mantle upon Elisha, it was a type of the anointing, meaning that it was the anointing that was qualifying Elisha for the work of the Lord. Over and over again we can observe how the anointing is what qualified men and women for the ministry. In the beginning of his ministry Moses was one who had the problem of looking at himself for qualifications instead of at God. After all the supernatural things he saw the day the Lord appeared to him, yet he still looked at himself and saw his own lack of ability.

The Word of God records how the anger of the Lord was kindled against him for this. "And Moses said unto the Lord, O my Lord, I am not eloquent, neither heretofore, nor since thou hast spoken unto thy servant: but I am slow of speech and of a slow tongue" (Ex. 4:10).

Now it is one thing to know that without the Lord you can do nothing. And it is another thing entirely to focus on your human weaknesses to the point that you cannot see the power of God that has qualified you for the ministry. At first Moses did not understand it was God who would be glorified in him because of the lack of ability on his part. But eventually he came to this understanding and learned to trust the power of God instead of looking at his lack of ability.

I believe there is a little bit of Moses in each one of us. As I said earlier, all of us have to come to grips with this lesson one way or another. Forty years prior to this time Moses had the opposite problem. He sensed the call of God but thought he could deliver the children of Israel in his own strength when he killed the Egyptian. As we know, it then took forty years on the backside of the desert for Moses to be emptied completely of himself so God could use him.

We can observe here that in every step of Moses' life he learned to be obedient to the life the Lord had for him as a minister. And so must we be obedient. Our Lord and Savior Jesus Christ fully understood this truth. For the Word of God tells us that when He came to the earth to fulfill God's plan He stripped Himself of all His power and depended entirely upon God.

Let this mind be in you, which was also in Christ Jesus: who, being in the form of God, thought it not robbery to be equal with God: but made himself of no reputation, and took upon him the form of a servant, and was made in the likeness of men: and being found in fashion as a man, he humbled himself, and became obedient unto death, even the death of the cross (Phil. 2:5-8).

Notice here that we are told to *think* the same way the Lord did when He was here on the earth. "Let this mind be in you." The Amplified Bible records, "Let this same attitude and purpose and humble mind be in you which was in Christ Jesus: (let Him be your example in humility)" (Phil. 2:5, Amp).

You see, though the Lord Jesus Christ was equal with God, yet the King James Version of the Bible records that

"He made himself of no reputation." That means Jesus stripped Himself of all His rights and privileges and power to become a man so the Father God could anoint Him and *qualify* Him for the ministry God had for Him.

This enabled our Lord to become obedient even unto death. Let's look at some other translations of this passage to get a clearer understanding of what is being taught here.

> **Have this attitude in yourselves, which was also in Christ Jesus, who, although He existed in the form of God, did not regard equality with God a thing to be grasped, but emptied Himself, taking the form of a bond-servant, and being made in the likeness of men. And being found in appearance as a man, He humbled Himself by becoming obedient to the point of death, even death on a cross (Phil. 2:5-8, NASB).**

> **For, let this mind be in you that is also in Christ Jesus, who, being in the form of God, thought it not robbery to be equal to God, but did empty himself, the form of a servant having taken, in the likeness of men having been made, and in fashion having been found as a man, humbled himself, having become obedient unto death—death even of a cross (Phil. 2:5-8, Young's Literal).**

> **Let the same mind be in you that was in Christ Jesus, who, though he was in the form of God, did not regard equality with God as something to be exploited, but emptied himself, taking the form of a slave, being born in human likeness. And being found in human form, he humbled himself and became obedient to the point of death—even death on a cross (Phil. 2:5-8, NRSV).**

And finally let's look at the Amplified Bible in these same verses.

Who, although being essentially one with God and in the form of God (possessing the fullness of the attributes which make God, God), did not think this equality with God was a thing to be eagerly grasped or retained, but stripped Himself (of all privileges and rightful dignity), so as to assume the guise of a servant (slave), in that He became like men and was born a human being. And after He had appeared in human form, He abased and humbled Himself (still further) and carried His obedience to the extreme of death, even the death of the cross (Phil. 2:6-8, Amp).

As our example our Lord taught us it is God the Father Himself who does all the qualifying. We can see this so clearly by the fact that Jesus didn't do any work of God until after He was anointed in the River Jordan and empowered by the Holy Spirit. Therefore all who have the call of God upon their lives need to know it is the Lord who calls them and equips them and qualifies them. When we understand this, all fear can go out the window. We will not have to look to any man for their ability to put us over.

We will then understand that because the Lord has qualified us we can do all things through Christ who is our strength. We can depend on His ability; His grace, His love and His wisdom for all that will come to us along the road of life. We can then rest in the Lord and watch Him enable us to do what we could not do in ourselves. Thank the Lord it is His call and it is His qualifications upon us as obedient ministers of the gospel.

Every minister must face the challenges of not only finding his place in ministry but also of learning to depend on the Lord for His ability and qualifications to do the ministry. Every type of minister must face these challenges. It doesn't matter if it's pastoral ministry or evangelism or the music ministry or the helps ministry. All of us must learn to depend on God's ability with which He has anointed us.

When Paul wrote to the Corinthians, he well understood these principles. He made it plain to all who would listen that it doesn't matter who the person is as the minister; what matters is that the minister be called and equipped to do the Lord's work.

For while one saith, I am of Paul; and another, I am of Apollos; are ye not carnal? Who then is Paul, and who is Apollos, but ministers by whom ye believed, even as the Lord gave to every man? I have planted, Apollos watered; but God gave the increase. So then neither is he that planteth any thing, neither he that watereth; but God that giveth the increase (1 Cor. 3:4-7).

The Corinthian church got caught up in the trap of the devil by putting too much emphasis on the personality of the minister. And, oh, how we realize this today in the body of Christ. Some in the church at Corinth thought the apostle Paul was not eloquent enough as a speaker. One thing common in Corinth was the theaters where individuals would compete for the position of most eloquent orator.

That spirit of competition actually got into the church. The church members began comparing the apostle Paul with Apollos, because it is in the fallen human nature of man to look at other men for their answers instead of at the Lord. Earlier in his letter to the Corinthians, Paul made mention that his preaching ministry was not with the wisdom of men. He wanted the church at Corinth to look to the power of God.

And I, brethren, when I came to you, came not with excellency of speech or of wisdom, declaring unto you the testimony of God. For I determined not to know any thing among you, save Jesus Christ, and him crucified. And I was with you in weakness, and in fear, and in much trembling. And my speech and my preaching were not with enticing words of man's wisdom, but in demonstration of the Spirit and of power: that your faith should not stand in the wisdom of men, but in the power of God (1 Cor. 2:1-5).

The apostle Paul did not depend on his ability to speak, though in the natural he could have done just that because of his education. He understood that all the natural ability one could muster would never compare to the power of God. That's why he told the church at Philippi that all those natural abilities he had were but dung.

For we are the circumcision, which worship God in the spirit, and rejoice in Christ Jesus, and have no confidence in the flesh. Though I might also have confidence in the flesh. If any other man thinketh that he hath whereof he might trust in the flesh, I more: circumcised the eighth day, of the stock of Israel, of the tribe of Benjamin, an Hebrew of the Hebrews; as touching the law, a Pharisee; concerning zeal, persecuting the church; touching the righteousness which is in the law, blameless. But what things were gain to me, those I counted loss for Christ. Yea, doubtless, and I count all things but loss for the excellency of the knowledge of Christ Jesus my Lord: for whom I have suffered the loss of all things, and do count them but dung, that I may win Christ (Phil. 3:3-8).

All those things that at one time were gain to Paul he now counted loss for Christ. You see, all of man's ability put together can never save one soul or heal one broken body or bring the peace of God into a troubled heart. But the power of God can. It is not a new program that will change the world. It is the power of God. It is ministering the love of God by the power of God to a sick and dying world that will make all the difference. So we must learn to depend on the one who has qualified us and put us into the ministry. That is the most important thing, depending on His anointing and power.

Every time I get behind a pulpit I am reminded of the fact that the Lord qualifies me. He must be the one who qualifies me for I have nothing to offer in myself. By remembering this truth we both keep ourselves from falling into pride, and we open the door for the Lord to manifest His power in us. If we fail to remember it is the Lord who qualifies us, then all that lies before us is a rocky road of anxiety. This is where we get into trouble! And this is why so many ministers go through burnout. Instead of depending on the power of the Lord to put them over, they try to do everything in their own strength.

That is exactly what King Saul did. He forgot it was the Lord who qualified him to be the king. And the end result was that he thought he was beyond being corrected by God. He was deceived in thinking he had the option to obey or disobey the will of God. The end result speaks for itself. What a tragedy! What a sad ending to a life that should have been blessed by God. But what happened to King Saul is an example to us all to remember that we are nothing without Him. It is the Lord who qualifies and will continue to qualify us if we keep our attitude and hearts right before Him. Never forget to depend on the qualifications you have been gifted with, so that at the end of the day the Lord Himself will receive all the glory.

III.

NOT I BUT CHRIST THAT LIVES IN ME

When we rest in the fact that it is the Lord who calls us and qualifies us it makes it easier to obey Him. We start by realizing that every obstacle, test or trial we face is another opportunity to let Him who has called and qualified us put us over.

Obedience to His call and plans becomes much easier by depending on the greater one who lives inside us. "I am crucified with Christ: nevertheless I live; yet not I, but Christ liveth in me: and the life which I now live in the flesh I live by the faith of the Son of God, who loved me, and gave himself for me" (Gal. 2:20, KJV).

Becoming inside minded instead of outside minded will help the minister in the walk of obedience. This is what the apostle Paul is talking about in the above verse of Scripture. And here is where obedience as a way of life comes in. For the temptation will come for us to gaze at everything around us instead of looking on the inside and by faith trusting the anointing to rise up within us.

I believe the greatest obstacle to our obedience to God is not the devil or other people or circumstances. I believe the greatest hindrance to the minister in his walk of obedience is the flesh. For the flesh desires its own way. It doesn't want to obey the Lord. It wants to be pampered and take the easy way out.

And here is where the minister must learn to obey the Lord's instructions about overcoming the flesh. For walking in the spirit is an act of obedience. Obeying the Word of God, walking in the spirit and living the life of love cannot be done without overcoming the flesh. And overcoming the flesh is such a personal walk of faith.

The apostle Paul understood the reality of the battle between the inward man and the outward man. In all of his epistles to the churches he taught something along this line because it is so important for the believer to overcome in this area. Let's look now at some of the things Paul taught about overcoming the flesh.

I do not understand my own actions. For I do not do what I want, but I do the very thing I hate. Now if I do what I do not want, I agree that the law is good. But in fact it is no longer I that do it, but sin that dwells within me. For I know that nothing good dwells within me, that is, in my flesh. I can will what is right, but I cannot do it.

For I do not do the good I want, but the evil I do not want is what I do. Now if I do what I do not want, it is no longer I that do it, but sin that dwells within me. So I find it to be a law that when I want to do what is good, evil lies close at hand. For I delight in the law of God in my inmost self,

**but I see in my members another law at war with
the law of my mind, making me captive to the law
of sin that dwells in my members (Rom. 7:19-23,
NRSV).**

Here is the greatest battle! You see, as born-again
believers we have the life and nature of God living on the
inside of us. But our bodies are not redeemed yet. Our flesh
still wants to do the wrong things. And this is why it is so
important to learn to walk in the spirit. If we walk in the flesh
we will never obey the Lord. And even though He desires to
bless us, He cannot do so to the extent He wants to because
we are not walking in the fullness of His will.

Every believer has the same battle to contend with that
Paul talked about in the above passage. But the minister has
a greater responsibility to walk in the spirit in order that he
may fulfill the call of God upon his or her life. Now let me
say here and now that the way has been provided for all of us
to *overcome* the flesh through our Lord Jesus Christ, as Paul
went on to declare in Romans 7 and 8.

Thank God we have the victory through the obedience
of our Lord. "Wretched man that I am! Who will rescue me
from this body of death? Thanks be to God through Jesus
Christ our Lord! So then, with my mind I am a slave to the
law of God, but with my flesh I am a slave to the law of sin"
(Rom. 7:24-25, NRSV).

You see, though the outward man still wants to serve the
law of sin, yet the life of God that lives in the inward man
will enable us to overcome the flesh with all its passions and
desires. This is where the minister must make the *decision* to
obey the Lord every day and not the dictates of the flesh.

Remember what the Lord said to the children of Israel
in the wilderness. "I call heaven and earth to witness against
you today that I have set before you life and death, blessings
and curses. Choose life so that you and your descendants

may live" (Deut. 30:19, NRSV). If the Jews back then had the ability to make the right decision, then how much more do we today?

So we overcome the flesh by the power of God that lives on the inside of our spirit. It is a walk of faith. It is a life of obedience. Rev. Kenneth E. Hagin makes a statement in his book *How You Can Be Led by the Spirit of God* that illustrates this battle.

> **Feeling is the voice of the body. Reason is the voice of the soul, or the mind. Conscience is the voice of the spirit. To go by feeling is to get into trouble. That is the reason so many Christians are up and down (I call them yo-yo Christians), and in and out. They go by their feelings. They don't walk by faith. They don't walk by their spirits. When they feel good they say, "Glory to God. Everything is fine." When they feel bad they say, I've lost it all (63).**

We cannot afford to listen to the voice of our body. For as Rev. Hagin said, "Feeling is the voice of the body." We must learn to obey our spirit. That's where the life of God abides.

That is where He will instruct us and guide us and lead us into every aspect of the ministry He has called us to. The obeying of our spirit is not a once-in-a-while affair. It is a way of life. Here is where we also learn obedience by the things we suffer.

Let's look now at what the apostle Paul said to the Galatians about walking in the spirit and overcoming the flesh. And as we do we will gain a clearer understanding of the importance of obeying the Lord in this area of our lives.

> **Live by the Spirit, I say, and do not gratify the desires of the flesh. For what the flesh desires is opposed to the Spirit, and what the Spirit desires**

is opposed to the flesh; for these are opposed to
each other, to prevent you from doing what you
want. But if you are led by the Spirit, you are not
subject to the law. Now the works of the flesh are
obvious: fornication, impurity, licentiousness,
idolatry, sorcery, enmities, strife, jealousy, anger,
quarrels, dissensions, factions, envy, drunkenness,
carousing, and things like these.

I am warning you, as I warned you before: those
who do such things will not inherit the kingdom
of God. By contrast, the fruit of the Spirit is love,
joy, peace, patience, kindness, generosity, faithfulness, gentleness, and self-control. There is no
law against such things. And those who belong
to Christ Jesus have crucified the flesh with its
passions and desires (Gal. 5:16-24, NRSV).

Oh, what a battle! Choosing every day and every moment
to obey the spirit and not the flesh! But we can do it by remembering what Paul remembered when he said, "I am crucified
with Christ" (Gal. 2:20, KJV). Once we come to the reality
that we are dead with Christ and alive unto God, we can then
allow Christ who lives in us to control our lives. And He will
do so. He will help us in every area of our lives to control the
flesh and yield to the Spirit. Laying down our life for Him
is the only way to live. This is a great paradox. Often ministers look everywhere for their fulfillment except to the cross
where they must learn they are crucified with Christ.

The power is available. The ability is available. And all
of heaven will back us up when we live the same kind of life
Jesus lived when He walked the earth. The power of God
will be released. And the Lord will be able to direct us into
the supernatural every day of our lives. We will no longer
be yo-yo Christians, as Rev. Hagin said. We won't live up

and down. But we will live a progressive and upward way of life where the Lord Jesus Christ is glorified. I know it is the deepest heart's desire in all of God's children to live and say, "Not I but Christ that lives in me."

Now let's talk about some practical illustrations in the life of the minister where understanding these principles is so important. Having been in the full-time ministry for twenty-five years I have observed that when ministers fail to allow Christ to live in them all sorts of problems surface.

Wrong attitudes develop to the point where they can be easily seen in the minister's life. And the more the minister tries to cover them, the more they show. Attitudes of competition, self-righteousness, pride and all the other works of the flesh will be the dominant factors. Instead of gaining our self-worth from Christ who has called us and anointed us, we look to the flesh for our self-worth.

Not one of us is immune to these temptations. I'm sure many ministers are hurting individuals because of trying to do the work of the ministry without allowing the greater One in them to do the work. It is time we as ministers become genuine with ourselves and real with all those to whom we minister. It is time we become genuine with each other and stop making ourselves out to be something we are not.

It is time to rest in who we are in Christ and just be ourselves so as to let our confidence be in the Lord and His Word, not in our ability in the flesh. We must rest in the gifts the Lord has placed in each one of us. We must learn to be satisfied with *our* calling and refuse to be someone else.

That's when peace will rule the day. That's when we can enjoy the work of the ministry. For then we will have come to the place where it doesn't matter what other people think. It doesn't matter whether we have the approval of others. The only thing that will matter is pleasing the Lord and obeying the call of God He has placed on our lives. Oh, what peace! Oh, what joy! Oh, what victory!

Andrew Murray states in his sermon "Dead to Self":

> **To have life in Himself is the prerogative of God alone, and of the Son, to whom the Father hath also given it. To seek life, not in itself, but in God, is the highest honor of the creature. To live in and to himself is the folly and guilt of sinful man; to live to God in Christ, the blessedness of the believer. To deny, to hate, to forsake, to lose his own life, such is the secret of the life of faith. "I live, yet not I, but Christ liveth in me"; "Not I, but the grace of God which is with me": this is the testimony of each one who has found out what it is to give up his own life, and to receive instead the blessed life of Christ within us. There is no other path to true life, to abiding in Christ, than that which our Lord went before us—through death.[1]**

I remember a number of years ago I asked the Lord in prayer to show me how to allow the life of God in me to be manifested on the outside. And I will never forget what He said to me. Of course everything He speaks to us will come directly from the Word of God.

When the Lord speaks so clearly to our hearts, He imparts a revelation that will abide with us forever. The first thing He said to me is recorded in Romans 12:1-2:

> **I appeal to you therefore, brothers and sisters, by the mercies of God, to present your bodies as a living sacrifice, holy and acceptable to God, which is your spiritual worship. Do not be conformed to this world, but be transformed by the renewing of your minds, so that you may discern what is the will of God—what is good and acceptable and perfect (Rom. 12:1-2, NRSV).**

He said to me that if the believer fails to act on this on a daily basis, then the flesh would begin to dominate. It is not something we do once in a while but every day of our lives, for the flesh is constantly waiting to control us if we do not crucify it by presenting it to Christ as a living sacrifice. In his book *How You Can Be Led by the Spirit of God* Rev. Hagin states the following that is so important for believers to comprehend and especially the minister who desires to obey God.

It is the inward man—not the outward man—that becomes a new creature in Christ. We still have the same body we had before we became a new creature. What we must learn to do is to let that new man on the inside of us dominate. With that new man, we control the flesh and do something with our bodies (17).

The next thing the Lord said to me was that we must "put on the new man by faith."

Again all of this is in the Word of God, but He said to me that this must be done every day.

He then directed me to the passage in Ephesians 4.

You were taught to put away your former way of life, your old self, corrupt and deluded by its lusts, and to be renewed in the spirit of your minds, and to clothe yourselves with the new self, created according to the likeness of God in true righteousness and holiness (Eph. 4:22-23, NRSV).

The King James Version of this passage says to "put on the new man." So first of all we must daily present our bodies to God a living sacrifice. Next we must put on the new man by faith. And then the Lord told me that we must follow after the fruit of the Spirit. That means by faith to actively pursue love, joy, peace, longsuffering, gentleness, meekness, faith and temperance.

By following after the fruit of the Spirit, we open the door for the anointing to manifest. The Lord once told me that by following after love, doors of divine appointment would open to me. So by allowing the life of God in us to manifest, it will bring with it all the things we desire to come to pass in our ministries. Again Andrew Murray in his sermon "Crucified With Christ" has some good thoughts along this line that are so relevant.

> **Taking up the cross was always spoken of by Christ as the test of discipleship. On three different occasions (Matt. 10:38, 16:24; Luke 14:27) we find the words repeated, "If any man will come after me, let him take up his cross and follow me." While the Lord was still on His way to the cross, this expression—taking up the cross—was the most appropriate to indicate that conformity to Him to which the disciple is called.[2]**

We are indeed called to take up our cross and follow Christ. This is a vital aspect of the call of God upon both the lives of ministers as well as believers. I remember the Lord once told me that "every act outside of love is yielding to a wrong spirit." Oh, how we have all yielded to the enemy more than we would like to admit. Rev. Murray continues by saying,

> **The believing disciple is himself crucified with Christ. The cross is the chief mark of the Christian as of Christ; the crucified Christ and the crucified Christian belong to each other. One of the chief elements of likeness to Christ consists in being**

crucified with Him. Whoever wishes to be like Him must seek to understand the secret of fellowship with His cross.[3]

This indeed is the suffering the believer is called to enter. And this is the suffering we are called to share in. It is saying no to the flesh with its affections and lusts. As believers we must understand that we cannot afford to open the door even a modest amount to the flesh. We cannot pet our flesh and let it have its way, for it will then dominate us.

The flesh cannot be reasoned with because the carnal mind is enmity against God. That is why we must crucify it. That is why we must not allow it to have its way in our lives, for it will always lead us away from Christ and His will for us. As Rev. Murray said, if we are to be like our Lord, then we must "understand the fellowship with His cross."

This fellowship with His cross is not something that is done once in awhile. We don't fellowship with His cross one day and allow our bodies to dominate us another day. No, it is a daily affair. It is a daily walking out of the will of God in our lives by saying no to the flesh and yes to the will of God.

We must present our bodies a living sacrifice to the Lord Jesus every day, and when we do so the power of the Lord to keep us is ours to depend upon. And the works of Jesus will then become our works as we labor for Him. We will learn it is not something to draw back from but something that becomes a joy to us.

---

[1]Thomas Nelson Inc., *Heritage of great evangelical teaching: Featuring the best of Martin Luther, John Wesley, Dwight L. Moody, C.H. Spurgeon and others [computer file], electronic ed., Logos Library System,* (Nashville: Thomas Nelson) 1997, c1996.

[2]Thomas Nelson Inc., *Heritage of great evangelical teaching: Featuring the best of Martin Luther, John Wesley, Dwight L. Moody, C.H. Spurgeon*

and others *[computer file], electronic ed., Logos Library System,* (Nashville: Thomas Nelson) 1997, c1996.

[3]Thomas Nelson Inc., *Heritage of great evangelical teaching: Featuring the best of Martin Luther, John Wesley, Dwight L. Moody, C.H. Spurgeon and others [computer file], electronic ed., Logos Library System,* (Nashville: Thomas Nelson) 1997, c1996.

IV.

BECOMING ALL THINGS TO ALL MEN

For though I be free from all men, yet have I made myself servant unto all, that I might gain the more. And unto the Jews I became as a Jew, that I might gain the Jews; to them that are under the law, as under the law, that I might gain them that are under the law; to them that are without law, as without law, (being not without law to God, but under the law to Christ,) that I might gain them that are without law. To the weak became I as weak, that I might gain the weak: I am made all things to all men, that I might by all means save some (1 Cor. 9:19-22).

Now we turn our attention to another aspect of the minister's life of obedience. And that is becoming all things to all men. What does this mean? Here lies the heartbeat of the called minister of God. As I stated earlier in this book, the ministry is not a chosen profession. It is a high calling. And it is a calling to serve other people as we serve the Lord Christ. Becoming all things to all men means that we identify with the peoples of the world. We don't judge them, for our Lord does not judge them.

And if any man hear my words, and believe not, I judge him not: for I came not to judge the world, but to save the world. He that rejecteth me, and receiveth not my words, hath one that judgeth him: the word that I have spoken, the same shall judge him in the last day (John 12:47-48).

We don't compromise with the sin of the world, but by the love of God we allow the reality of the Holy Spirit to be seen in us. Many believers and indeed many ministers have not learned obedience in this area of life. Obedience to God will mean loving the loveless, feeding the hungry and identifying with everyone regardless of their social status or financial status in life. Here is the very heart of our Lord's ministry when He was upon the earth. And now it should be the very heartbeat of our ministry as we continue His work upon the earth.

The King James Version Study Bible makes an interesting note here.

One of the results of redemption is the liberty of the believer. Christians are free from depending on the law and free from the bondage of their old nature. Christian liberty releases us to accomplish all our potential. But that liberty should not be abused to justify hedonistic behavior. Although believers live in a state of freedom, concern for reaching others with the gospel and helping weaker believers grow will result in voluntary self-restraint in areas

that might offend others, or hinder our efforts in reaching and helping people.[4]

When we accept Jesus as our personal Lord and Savior we gain the liberty of being made free from all men. But this is where the love of God comes in. By yielding to the love of God that is in our hearts we will actually allow the power of God to be ministered to a sick and dying world. Verse 19 in the Amplified Bible reads, "For although I am free in every way from anyone's control, I have made myself a bondservant to everyone, so that I might gain the more (for Christ)." All hypocrisies disappear when we become all things to all men. The pride of life disappears when we become all things to all men. Church politics disappear when we become all things to all men.

All the works of the law disappear when we become all things to all men. Indeed the very center of our beings is measured by this standard—becoming all things to all men. We can see how Jesus practiced this every day in His earthly ministry. Everywhere He went He saw the need of man and endeavored to lift him up out of that need.

He wasn't afraid to talk to the Samaritan woman, even though the Jews had no dealings with the Samaritans. He was not afraid to heal the lepers. He didn't care that He was known to keep company with sinners. He loved the rich, and He loved the homeless.

Jesus treated all peoples with equality regardless of who they were. But He was quick to speak out against hypocrisy. Over and over again He demonstrated that He loved the people while hating all forms of hypocrisy.

"Therefore when thou doest thine alms, do not sound a trumpet before thee, as the hypocrites do in the synagogues and in the streets, that they may have glory of men. Verily I say unto you, they have their reward" (Matt. 6:2, KJV).

Notice that Jesus said the hypocrite loves to receive the glory of men.

The minister who becomes all things to all men cannot be a hypocrite. People know when someone is real with them or if that individual is putting up a front. It all comes down to the motive of the heart. If our hearts are right, we will walk in purity with all men. And others will be able to visualize that reality as surely as one can see the sun that rises in the east.

Again borrowing from Andrew Murray's sermon titled "Humility in Daily Life," we will find some interesting truths that must be dealt with in the minister's life of obedience.

> **What a solemn thought, that our love to God will be measured by our everyday intercourse with men and the love it displays; and that our love to God will be found to be a delusion, except as its truth is proved in standing the test of daily life with our fellow-men. It is even so with our humility. It is easy to think we humble ourselves before God: humility towards men will be the only sufficient proof that our humility before God is real; that humility has taken up its abode in us, and become our very nature; that we actually, like Christ, have made ourselves of no reputation. When in the presence of God lowliness of heart has become, not a posture we assume for a time, when we think of Him, or pray to Him, but the very spirit of our life, it will manifest itself in all our bearing towards our brethren.[5]**

He states "our love to God will be measured by our everyday intercourse with men." And there cannot be a truer statement. Remember what the Word of God tells us in the epistle of 1 John?

**If a man say, I love God, and hateth his brother, he
is a liar: for he that loveth not his brother whom
he hath seen, how can he love God whom he hath
not seen? And this commandment have we from
him, that he who loveth God loveth his brother
also. Whosoever believeth that Jesus is the Christ
is born of God: and every one that loveth him that
begat loveth him also that is begotten of him (1
John 4:20, 21–5:1).**

Becoming all things to all men is determined by the very
center of thought and action. It is not a fleeting compassion for our fellowman. It is a way of life that grows out
of our relationship with God the Father Himself. When the
very nature of Christ possesses us to the point that we also
are moved with His compassion, then we will become all
things to all men. Andrew Murray continued in his sermon
on humility by saying,

**Is not this what Jesus taught? It was when the
disciples disputed who should be greatest; when
He saw how the Pharisees loved the chief place
at feasts and the chief seats in the synagogues;
when He had given them the example of washing
their feet—that He taught His lessons of humility.
Humility before God is nothing if not proved in
humility before men.[6]**

This kind of obedience does not come about because one
is told to do so. It cannot be a reality in our lives because
of some code of conduct. It must be a part of the minister's
life because of the maintenance of a perfect heart based on
one's relationship and fellowship with the Lord Jesus Christ
Himself. It is the love of God flowing out of us to those who

need it the most. It is God's love and mercy and Word in action through vessels of honor.

The reality of becoming all things to all men doesn't mean that everyone we meet who is lost will necessarily give their life to the Lord. Paul said, "I am made all things to all men, that I might by all means save some" (1 Cor. 9:22, KJV). He knew that not all would be saved, but he also knew that some would be saved.

Oh, how we see so much competition in the body of Christ today both among churches and ministers. It seems that the church has lost its motivation to win the lost by becoming motivated by greed. It seems that success is now measured by a church's bank account. Everywhere we may look, we see such merchandising of the gospel. Remember this passage:

> **Then Jesus entered the temple and drove out all who were selling and buying in the temple, and he overturned the tables of the money changers and the seats of those who sold doves. He said to them, "It is written, 'My house shall be called a house of prayer'; but you are making it a den of robbers (Matt. 21:12-13, NRSV).**

It seems as if history has repeated itself when you notice the number of churches and ministries selling so many things in the church or on television. I fully understand that it takes money to finance the gospel, but there is a fine line between giving people an opportunity to give and becoming focused on making money.

There is a fine line between using money for the gospel and becoming greedy. Remember that the Word says that it isn't money, but "the love of money is the root of all evil: which while some coveted after, they have erred from the faith, and pierced themselves through with many sorrows" (1

Tim. 6:10, KJV). There is nothing wrong with money. As I have said, it takes lots of money to do the work of the ministry. But the temptation to become greedy is so enormous that the minister must guard his heart and judge his motives to be sure the reason he is in the ministry is a pure one.

Moreover that motive should be the salvation of the world. We must also guard our attitude toward the poor in our churches, and see to it that we do not prefer the wealthy to the poor.

My brothers and sisters, do you with your acts of favoritism really believe in our glorious Lord Jesus Christ? For if a person with gold rings and in fine clothes comes into your assembly, and if a poor person in dirty clothes also comes in, and if you take notice of the one wearing the fine clothes and say, "Have a seat here, please," while to the one who is poor you say, "Stand there," or, "Sit at my feet," have you not made distinctions among yourselves, and become judges with evil thoughts (James 2:1-2, NRSV).

And yet such sinful preference is seen everywhere in the body of Christ. As ministers we need to remember that many are watching us in what we say and do. Many in the body of Christ will follow our lead. If we show favoritism, as a great leaven it will spread in the church. Indeed this is one of the very signs of the last days recorded in the Word of God by the apostle Peter.

But there were false prophets also among the people, even as there shall be false teachers among you, who privily shall bring in damnable heresies, even denying the Lord that bought them, and bring upon themselves swift destruction. And

many shall follow their pernicious ways; by reason of whom the way of truth shall be evil spoken of. And through covetousness shall they with feigned words make merchandise of you: whose judgment now of a long time lingereth not, and their damnation slumbereth not (2 Pet. 2:1-3, KJV).

Notice that Peter said these false prophets will "make merchandise of you:"

That word "merchandise" is very interesting in the original Greek. Let's take a look at it. This is the definition: "*emporeuomai, em-por-yoo'-om-ahee;* from G1722 and G4198; to travel in (a country as a peddler), i.e. (by impl.) to trade:—buy and sell, make merchandise" (Strong's Hebrew Greek Dictionary).

To travel as a peddler, to trade, buy and sell! Think of it! Do we not see this happening in our churches today? But by becoming all things to all men our hearts as ministers remain pure before God. For our motivation will not be how much money we can make but rather how many people can we win to Jesus? Don't misunderstand me! I believe it is God's will to bless the minister as he or she obeys the call of God upon his or her life. Indeed the Word of God is clear that it is God's will to bless us financially. As I have said, it's not the money that is wrong; it is the *love* of money that is the root of all evil.

Oh, how the enemy would try to destroy good ministries by drawing them away from the right motive for ministry. Many have fallen because of the lust of the flesh or the pride of life.

People will try to put the minister up on a pedestal in order to get them to fall into pride. Satan knows that if he can destroy one minister he has hurt many others at the same time.

"For all that is in the world, the lust of the flesh, and the lust of the eyes, and the pride of life, is not of the Father, but is of the world. And the world passeth away, and the lust thereof: but he that doeth the will of God abideth forever" (1 John 2:16-17, KJV). We must never forget that Jesus said, "The Spirit of the Lord is upon me, because he hath anointed me to preach the gospel to the poor; he hath sent me to heal the brokenhearted, to preach deliverance to the captives, and recovering of sight to the blind, to set at liberty them that are bruised" (Luke 4:18, KJV). Motive is everything in the kingdom of God. Everything we are or will ever be begins with the right motive. And only our Father knows if we are maintaining the right motive or not. Men can only see the outward appearance, but the Lord sees the heart. His eyes are constantly searching the deepest cavity in the hearts of men.

Borrowing again from Andrew Murray in his sermon "Humility in Daily Life" we can find that the man who walks in humility can prefer others ahead of himself.

The humble man feels no jealousy or envy. He can praise God when others are preferred and blessed before him. He can bear to hear others praised and himself forgotten, because in God's presence he has learned to say with Paul, "I am nothing." He has received the spirit of Jesus, who pleased not Himself, and sought not His own honor, as the spirit of his life.

Amid what are considered the temptations to impatience and touchiness, to hard thoughts and sharp words, which come from the failings and sins of fellow-Christians, the humble man carries the oft-repeated injunction in his heart, and shows it in his life, *"Forbearing one another, and forgiving one another, even as the Lord forgave you."* He has learned that in putting on the Lord Jesus he *has put on the heart of compassion, kindness, humility, meekness, and long-suffering.*[7]

Rev. Charles Spurgeon in his sermon "Qualifications for Soul Winning" states the following: "You must have a real desire for the good of the people if you are to have much influence over them. Why, even dogs and cats love the people who love them, and human beings are much the same as these dumb animals. People very soon get to know when a cold man gets into the pulpit, one of those who seem to have been carved out of a block of marble."[8]

Let it not be said of the minister that he or she has been carved out of marble. Let it be said of us as ministers instead "there is someone who really loves the unlovable." Let all who have been called into the ministry ask themselves, "Have I become all things to all men that I may by all means win some?"

William Baxter makes the following statement in his book *The Reformed Pastor:* "Though men strive and reach for those offices of honor, I have seldom seen men strive so furiously about being first at a poor man's cottage in order to teach him and his family the way to heaven. Or indeed I have not seen men compete to be first to bring a soul to Christ, or to become the servant of all. It is strange that for all the plain teachings of Christ, men will not understand the nature of their office! If they did, they would strive to be the pastor of a whole county and more where there are ten thousand poor sinners needing help" (87).

This can only be done when we allow Christ to live in us. This cannot be done when we love the praises of men more than the praises of God. Only Christ in us the hope of glory can motivate us to travel the extra mile and lay down our lives for the brethren. Only by His grace and His anointing and His ability can we do what we in ourselves cannot do.

The challenge is great, but the rewards are eternal. The battle over the flesh is great, but the victory is sweet. That is what our Lord meant when He said, "If we lose our life we will find it" (Matt.16:25). If our motive for living and doing what we do as ministers is simply to gratify our flesh, then we are truly miserable men.

This is one reason why we need constant renewals of the Holy Spirit. Jesus Himself said, "The spirit indeed is willing, but the flesh is weak" (Matt. 26:41). Only a person with total dependency on the Lord and a consecrated heart filled with His love can become all things to all men. It is so easy to forget these things and slip into complacency, but we must not. The cry of our heart should be, "Lord, help me to help others this day as I may not pass this way again."

---

[4]Thomas Nelson Inc., *King James Version Study Bible [computer file]*, *electronic ed., Logos Library System*, (Nashville: Thomas Nelson) 1997, c1988 by Liberty University.

[5]Thomas Nelson Inc., *Heritage of great evangelical teaching: Featuring the best of Martin Luther, John Wesley, Dwight L. Moody, C.H. Spurgeon and others [computer file], electronic ed., Logos Library System*, (Nashville: Thomas Nelson) 1997, c1996.

[6]Thomas Nelson Inc., *Heritage of great evangelical teaching: Featuring the best of Martin Luther, John Wesley, Dwight L. Moody, C.H. Spurgeon and others [computer file], electronic ed., Logos Library System*, (Nashville: Thomas Nelson) 1997, c1996.

[7]Thomas Nelson Inc., *Heritage of great evangelical teaching: Featuring the best of Martin Luther, John Wesley, Dwight L. Moody, C.H. Spurgeon and others [computer file], electronic ed., Logos Library System*, (Nashville: Thomas Nelson) 1997, c1996.

[8]Thomas Nelson Inc., *Heritage of great evangelical teaching: Featuring the best of Martin Luther, John Wesley, Dwight L. Moody, C.H. Spurgeon and others [computer file], electronic ed., Logos Library System*, (Nashville: Thomas Nelson) 1997, c1996.

V.

MAINTAINING A SERVANT'S HEART OF OBEDIENCE

M aintaining a servant's heart of compassion goes hand in hand with knowing no man after the flesh. The minister's life of obedience is one of a servant. To live beyond oneself in a life of giving is what the ministry is all about. All of us are called to be servants whether we are called to the full-time ministry or not. The word "servant" comes from the Greek word *douloo*, which means, "to enslave literally or figuratively" (Strong's Hebrew Greek Dictionary). The call to the ministry is a call to service. A call to serve our Lord and perform His will here on the earth.

> **Know ye not, that to whom ye yield yourselves servants to obey, his servants ye are to whom ye obey; whether of sin unto death, or of obedience unto righteousness? But God be thanked, that ye were the servants of sin, but ye have obeyed**

from the heart that form of doctrine which was delivered you. Being then made free from sin, ye became the servants of righteousness (Rom. 6:16-18).

When we were lost we were the servants of sin. But I am thankful we are now free from sin and have become the servants of righteousness. I don't believe the body of Christ understands what it means to be a servant. Especially in the West we know little about the virtue of servant hood. We have become a society much like the old Roman Empire, where everyone lived for self and pleasure. We don't perceive what it means to sacrifice anything. We don't know what it means to be without. We don't comprehend what it means to lay down our rights for the sake of someone else. But that is what being a servant is all about.

It is doing the things that are not always convenient. It is doing things that require sacrifice and patient love. It is recognizing that what we do to others we are really doing to Christ.

Ours has become a life of ease where we expect everything to be handed to us on a silver platter. So the attitude and spirit that is in the world has gotten into the church. The very thing that made Rome fall is creeping into every nook and cranny of society. It's becoming increasingly difficult to find men and women of honor who are willing to lay down their lives for each other.

And yet that is exactly what the New Testament teaches us, to know the reality that what we do to others we are really doing to the Lord Jesus Christ. He was our example in being a servant to the extreme, even the extreme of the cross.

But made himself of no reputation, and took upon him the form of a servant, and was made in the likeness of men: and being found in fashion as a

man, he humbled himself, and became obedient unto death, even the death of the cross (Phil. 2:7-8).

Likewise, we are commanded to have the same attitude of servant hood to the point that we are willing to lay down our lives for the brethren. "Hereby perceive we the love of God, because he laid down his life for us: and we ought to lay down our lives for the brethren" (1 John 3:16). It is so interesting to note that it is John 3:16 which tells us God so loved the world that He gave His only begotten Son. And here in 1 John 3:16 we are told to lay down our lives for the brethren. Can we do it? I believe we can! Are we willing to do it? That is the heart of the question and at the very heart of the minister.

Indeed the very breath and nature of God that reside in each of us give us the desire and motivation and ability to live such a life of service. But this life of service requires sacrifice. And here is where the church has become lazy in its commitment to the gospel. I believe this is the hour when we need to wake up and be challenged in this area.

I'm also convinced a great number of believers and ministers in the body of Christ are servants of righteousness. At times, though, these individuals live in obscurity against the backdrop of a selfish world. But praise the Lord they are there, working and living for righteousness and giving themselves unselfishly day and night. These are the real heroes in this world.

And they are making a difference. The kingdom of God is growing every day, and the end of the age is near when our Lord will return and judge according to the secrets of men's hearts. The unselfish sacrifice of fathers and mothers and children is making the mark of Jesus spread all over this world. Thank the Lord there are those who are not afraid to humble themselves and become servants.

Many faithful men and women are serving our Lord in the most remote places of the earth, where little thanks is given except by those hungry souls who are being fed both physically and spiritually. We need to lift these people up in prayer every day that great fruit will spring forth from their loving service.

But the challenge to all of us who are called by the name of Christ is to resist the temptation to become complacent and selfish. We must rise above the desires of the flesh to be reminded again what it means to serve without thought of being recognized by anyone except our Lord. The challenge is great, but so is the One who lives on the inside of us. He has called and He has equipped and He will provide all we need to succeed as servants.

God's grace and power are released as we stand up to the task that lies ahead of us. Is it always easy? No! Is it rewarding? Most certainly, yes, it is. It is the most rewarding thing in the world to know that by becoming servants with hearts of compassion many will be saved from a devil's hell. What more reward is there?

And there was also a strife among them, which of them should be accounted the greatest. And he said unto them, The kings of the Gentiles exercise lordship over them; and they that exercise authority upon them are called benefactors. But ye shall not be so: but he that is greatest among you, let him be as the younger; and he that is chief, as he that doth serve (Luke 22:24-26).

Jesus made it clear that the greatest in the kingdom of God is the one who serves others. And here is where we must guard our hearts as ministers, for as I discussed in earlier chapters it is the flesh that desires to be pampered. It wants its way. It doesn't want to sacrifice. So this is a daily battle.

It is a fight of faith. It is a life of love. It is a way of life for the minister who wants to please his Lord more than anything else. God the Father will honor those who choose to serve the Lord with all their heart. The honor that comes from God is worth more than the entire honor that man could muster in a million years.

"Whoever serves me must follow me, and where I am, there will my servant be also. Whoever serves me, the Father will honor" (John 12:26, NRSV). Notice our Savior said that the one who would serve the Lord must follow the Lord. That means following His Word and Spirit and the leading of the Spirit into those places where we can be the greatest blessing. All the while knowing and recognizing that He will provide and make possible all He has placed in our hearts to do for Him. This is what Jesus meant when He said that many are called but few are chosen. Few make the decision to follow the Lord into those places where it isn't easy. But the apostle Paul did just that.

And the glory of the Lord was manifested on him and through him as many believed on Jesus and were born again. That's why Paul said to follow him as he followed Christ.

And when he had begun to reckon, one was brought unto him, which owed him ten thousand talents. But forasmuch as he had not to pay, his lord commanded him to be sold, and his wife, and children, and all that he had, and payment to be made. The servant therefore fell down, and worshipped him, saying, Lord, have patience with me, and I will pay thee all. Then the lord of that servant was moved with compassion, and loosed him, and forgave him the debt. But the same servant went out, and found one of his fellowservants, which owed him an hundred pence: and he laid hands on him, and took him by the throat,

saying, Pay me that thou owest. And his fellowservant fell down at his feet, and besought him, saying, Have patience with me, and I will pay thee all. And he would not: but went and cast him into prison, till he should pay the debt.

So when his fellowservants saw what was done, they were very sorry, and came and told unto their lord all that was done. Then his lord, after that he had called him, said unto him, O thou wicked servant, I forgave thee all that debt, because thou desiredst me: Shouldest not thou also have had compassion on thy fellowservant, even as I had pity on thee? (Matt. 18:24-33).

How much has the Lord forgiven us? The debt we owed could never have been paid in a million lifetimes. And this is what our Lord is talking about in the above passage of Scripture. We ought to have compassion on our fellow servant. It never ceases to amaze me how so often when individuals in the body of Christ need help they are persecuted instead.

Often this persecution comes from within our own ranks instead of the world. But compassion is what our heavenly Father is looking for in our lives. Compassion is what compels us to go into the entire world and preach the gospel to every creature. And it is the Lord's compassion that lives in us.

That's why we can take credit for nothing. The call is His. The qualifications are His. And the compassion is His. But we as ministers must obey that compassion and yield to it. For it is there. Down deep in the innermost parts of the heart are the love of God and the compassion of God. But we must choose to release them.

In a day in which it was quite common to have servants, the apostles had little difficulty in understanding the concept of being servants for the Lord. Over and over again when they addressed the churches they referred to themselves as "servants" of Jesus Christ. Notice the following:

> **Paul, a servant of Jesus Christ, called to be an apostle, separated unto the gospel of God (Rom. 1:1, KJV).**

> **I commend unto you Phebe our sister, which is a servant of the church which is at Cenchrea (Rom. 16:1, KJV).**

> **Epaphras, who is one of you, a servant of Christ, saluteth you (Col. 4:12, KJV).**

> **Paul, a servant of God, and an apostle of Jesus Christ, according to the faith of God's elect (Titus 1:1, KJV).**

> **James, a servant of God and of the Lord Jesus Christ, to the twelve tribes which are scattered abroad, greeting (James 1:1, KJV).**

> **Simon Peter, a servant and an apostle of Jesus Christ, to them that have obtained like precious faith with us through the righteousness of God and our Saviour Jesus Christ (2 Pet. 1:1, KJV).**

> **Jude, the servant of Jesus Christ, and brother of James, to them that are sanctified by God the Father, and preserved in Jesus Christ, and called (Jude 1, KJV).**

Are you beginning to get the picture? Oh, how refreshing it would be to hear ministers today refer to themselves as servants of Jesus Christ. All too often today it's the title ministers want to flash around as if to say, "Look at me. I'm something special." What's more—many in the body of Christ will go to the greatest lengths to sit under such ministers. It is time ministers pick up again the attitude of being servants in this world, not stars; to serve rather than wanting to be served. Oh, how refreshing it would be indeed.

For God is my witness, whom I serve with my spirit in the gospel of his Son, that without ceasing I make mention of you always in my prayers; making request, if by any means now at length I might have a prosperous journey by the will of God to come unto you. For I long to see you, that I may impart unto you some spiritual gift, to the end ye may be established (Rom. 1:9-11).

Notice in the above passage that the apostle Paul said, "I serve with my spirit." Herein lies the key to serving with a heart of compassion. Serving must come from the heart. Notice also that, as a direct result of Paul's heart to serve, he desired to impart spiritual gifts to the Roman believers so they would be established. This is the very heart of the Father God Himself. Oh, how we can see this servant's heart in the life and ministry of our Lord Jesus Christ.

So after he had washed their feet, and had taken his garments, and was set down again, he said unto them, Know ye what I have done to you? Ye call me Master and Lord: and ye say well; for so I am. If I then, your Lord and Master, have washed your feet; ye also ought to wash one another's feet (John 13:12-14).

Here our Lord not only humbled Himself to the point where He washed the disciples' feet, but He further used this example to teach what it means to have a servant's heart of compassion. Here we are taught that all-important difference between the body of Christ and the rest of the world.

The world doesn't understand these concepts, for they are in the kingdom of darkness. You see all sin is *selfishness*. That is what made Lucifer fall in the first place. He wanted his way at the expense of everyone else. And he is still trying to destroy everyone he can to further his kingdom. But in the church it is just the opposite. We are governed by the rule of love.

It takes the life and nature of God to wash another man's feet, both literally and figuratively. No other kingdom can do this. No other law that has ever been passed can make people do this. In the world it is dog-eat-dog. Walking on someone else to get to the top is the way of the world, but not so in the kingdom of heaven.

In the Old Testament the high priest would take a bath in the bathhouse outside the tabernacle. But before he could go into the presence of God he had to wash his feet again. This was possible for there was a laver filled with water and placed outside the holy place. So from the bathhouse to the holy place the high priest would pick up some dirt on his feet and therefore had to wash his feet again.

This is what our Lord was teaching His disciples. They were already clean by the Word that was spoken to them. But on life's journey we tend to pick up some dirt and need to have Jesus wash our feet again. In other words if Jesus cleanses and forgives us, we ought to do the same with each other.

SERVING THE LORD WITHOUT A
SERVANT'S HEART

Many in the body of Christ know what it means to "serve" the Lord. But the question is, are they doing so with a servant's heart? You see, staying busy for the Lord is not enough. Just doing things for the "ministry" is not enough. Doing the right things and going the right places are not enough.

And this is what many ministers fall into. They stay busy for the Lord and get burned out because their hearts are not in what they are doing. Remember the example of this principle in the Word of God. The story is found in Luke's Gospel. Let's take a look at this passage to learn some important principles of serving the Lord from the heart.

> **Now it came to pass, as they went, that he entered into a certain village: and a certain woman named Martha received him into her house. And she had a sister called Mary, which also sat at Jesus' feet, and heard his word. But Martha was cumbered about much serving (Luke 10:38-40).**

Here Martha was cumbered about much serving. The Greek work translated "cumbered" here is *perispao*, and it means, "to drag all around" (Strong's Hebrew Greek Dictionary). In other words, though Martha was doing the right things, most of which were necessary, yet her heart was not in what she was doing, and it became a drag to her.

Does this sound familiar? We can be busy for Jesus while our hearts are far from Him. Now not only did Martha get weary serving the Lord, she began to find fault with Mary and judged her based on what she was doing. Notice the rest of the story.

> **...and came to him, and said, Lord, dost thou not care that my sister hath left me to serve alone? Bid her therefore that she help me. And Jesus answered and said unto her, Martha, Martha, thou art careful and troubled about many things: But one thing is needful: and Mary hath chosen**

that good part, which shall not be taken away from her (Luke 10:40-42).

Notice the response of Jesus to Martha. He said, "One thing is needful." And that will never change. We must spend time at the feet of Jesus so that His heart of compassion will saturate us more and more. Becoming completely enveloped in His love and compassion for others comes by simply spending time in the presence of Jesus.

Therefore if we are going to keep our priorities in the proper perspective, by understanding that what is *in* us will come *out* of us, then we must not get overly busy with the duties of the ministry and forget the heart of the ministry. We must never lose our compassion for people, and that means all people from all walks of life and backgrounds.

DON'T BECOME ANOTHER MARTHA

We can get so busy with the everyday affairs of life that we slip into the same attitude Martha had. None of us is immune to this possibility. None of us can say it could never happen to me. You see, the key is maintaining that servant's heart that was given to us at the moment of salvation.

Losing the servant's heart of obedience doesn't happen overnight anymore than backsliding happens overnight. But little by little other things will draw us away from the attitude Jesus wants us to have on a continual basis. It's a matter of maintaining the basic things in the Christian life like prayer, reading the Word of God and staying in fellowship with the Lord and fellow believers.

It involves work, patience and the constant refusal to let down our guard to the traps of the enemy of our souls. It involves sitting at the feet of Jesus and hearing His Word as Mary did. This indeed is what makes us as believers different from the world. It is the life and nature of our Lord living in us on a daily basis.

VI.

WALKING IN INTEGRITY

Who shall abide in thy tabernacle? who shall dwell
in thy holy hill? **He that walketh uprightly, and
worketh righteousness, and speaketh the truth in
his heart. He that backbiteth not with his tongue,
nor doeth evil to his neighbour, nor taketh up a
reproach against his neighbour.**

**In whose eyes a vile person is contemned; but
he honoureth them that fear the LORD. He that
sweareth to his own hurt, and changeth not (Ps.
15:1-4).**

What does it mean to walk in integrity? The above
passage gives us some light on the subject. God says
the righteous man "swears to his own hurt, and changes not."
In other words, the righteous man keeps his word even if it
costs him. It means to be a man or woman of your word.

It means to put the virtue of honesty above one's self-
interest. It means placing more value on having the Lord's
approval than man's approval. It means being able to lie down

at night knowing you have wronged no man. It means doing the right thing even when nobody knows it but the Lord.

There can be no such thing as a minister's life of obedience without a life of integrity. Oh, how we need men and women who will walk in integrity. Today, however, we live in a world where the principles of honesty and integrity have not been taught. As a result we see such a lack of morals.

It may seem to the individual that a small act of dishonesty may not hurt anyone, but every act of dishonesty hurts everybody. It creeps into every corner of society to cause every low product of the fallen nature of man to manifest itself to the destroying of society. When it comes to integrity in the ministry, it is sad to say that there is a deficit.

Among those who should be the very examples of integrity all too often we see compromise and greed of the highest order. I don't want to imply that all ministers are crooks. Thank the Lord there are still those who place a high value on the virtue of integrity.

But this book is to stir up those of us who are called, qualified and anointed to do the work of the ministry. It is to remind us of our great moral and spiritual obligation to do the right thing even if it may seem to hurt us. For in the end we know the eyes of the Lord are over the righteous. And it means more to us to have the approval of Him who knows all things.

Rev. Kenneth Copeland makes a statement in his book *Honor: Walking in Honesty, Truth and Integrity* that "some of the most dishonorable things I have seen in the latter years of my life have come from Christians—Christian teachers and preachers" (30).

What a sad statement! But I have found the same thing to be true in my observation of ministers' lives over the years. We can't do anything, though, about those who would compromise their integrity, but we can purpose in our hearts by the power of the Holy Spirit not to violate our own hearts and to be men and women of integrity.

Does it matter? Yes, it does! Will it pay in the long run to walk in this kind of righteousness? Yes, indeed, for the day will surely come when we will reap what we have sown. "For promotion cometh neither from the east, nor from the west, nor from the south. But God is the judge: he putteth down one, and setteth up another" (Ps. 75:6-7, KJV). In the end the man or woman of integrity will inherit the earth. Those are the individuals who will be promoted by the Lord. And all those who desire the blessing of the Lord would have it no other way.

I want to share with you an experience I had with the Lord when I was in Bible school back in 1980. I was attending Rhema Bible Training Center in Broken Arrow, Oklahoma. I worked part-time and went to school full-time. I worked in downtown Tulsa at Amoco Production Company at that time in their computer library. Since I worked the midnight shift, I usually tried to get a nap on Sunday afternoon so I could make it through the night and be awake in my class the next morning.

One Sunday afternoon, while I was taking a nap, the Lord visited me. And He did so in a dream. As I teach everywhere I go, there are three sources of dreams. The Lord can give you a dream. The devil can give you a dream. And then there is what I call pizza dreams. You know, that's where you ate the wrong thing before going to bed and then dream all sorts of crazy things.

Well, this dream came from the Lord. I remember sensing such an overwhelming desire to do the will of God, but I didn't know where to go or how to get there. I saw myself in a large open area with nothing but the call of God upon my life. I can't describe in words how strong that desire was. I can simply state that it was the only thing important to me then, to know and obey that call on my life.

While looking for a way to go I saw a picture of the United States. It was huge, as if I were looking on a great wall. I saw a hand draw a straight line from Tulsa to my home in West Virginia, and then the map disappeared. After this I found myself in a bus station where a bus pulled up beside me and opened its door. The driver proceeded to tell me he was going that way and could get me there faster than anyone could.

As I took the first step on the bus thinking this had to be my ride, the driver said, "But I'll break the law doing it." I remember stepping off that bus saying, "Sorry, I can't go with you." The driver said, "Find your own way then," and slammed the door and left.

I began looking for a way to get there again. You see, "there" was the will of God. At least that was what it meant to me. Again I looked and saw another picture of the United States on that great wall and again a hand drawing a line from Tulsa to West Virginia. Only this time instead of a straight line, I saw a crooked line.

After that map had disappeared, I found myself in a bank thinking, *Maybe I can borrow the money to get there.* As the bank was full of people, I waited my turn in one of the teller lines to try to find out who the loan officer was and to ask about getting the financial help I needed.

While standing in that line, a man I had never met before began to falsely accuse me of being a liar and a thief. I remember feeling so shocked as every eye in that bank was on me. That man became violent to the point that he tried to jump me when the bank president escorted me away into his office.

He started to call the police, believing I was a trouble-maker, when I told him to look me in the eye. As he did so the anointing of God came on me, and I began to preach to him about Jesus and the call of God upon my life. I told him why I was there and that I was just trying to find a way to obey God and get where He wanted me to go.

The bank president stood up and put his arm on my shoulder and said, "Don't worry about it, Mr. Richards. I'll take care of it." Then I woke up, and the power and presence of the Lord was so thick in that room it seemed you could have cut it with a knife. I remember not wanting to move because the holiness of God was in that place.

So I waited there on the side of my bed, not wanting to move, when I heard the Lord say to me, "Go get a pen and paper and write this down. I'm going to give you the interpretation of what you just saw."

First, He told me the desire to get to my home represented the call of God upon my life. The large map of the United States with the straight line drawn on it represented "the quick and easy way." He proceeded to tell me I would be tempted to take the quick and easy way, which was represented by the bus driver who said he could get me there but would break the law in doing it.

The Lord told me the quick and easy way was the "way of no integrity" and I was not to take that way. The map with the crooked line represented the Lord's will for me. Though it would not be quick or easy, it was the "way of integrity."

The Lord told me the man in the bank who falsely accused me represented those who would be used by the devil to try to persecute me by lying about me. The bank president represented those the Lord would give me favor with who would help me get the job done.

Over the years I've observed most of this prophecy as it has come to pass. But the principles the Lord taught me belong to everyone. The devil's path may seem quick. But it will always require compromising our integrity to follow that path. In the end do we really want what the world calls success at the expense of our walk with the Lord? I don't think so.

I remember Rev. Kenneth E. Hagin telling us as students in Bible school that "God doesn't always settle up on every

Saturday night, but sooner or later He settles up." It may look as if it is costing you to walk in integrity, but in the end it will always pay rich dividends.

"For the eyes of the Lord run to and fro throughout the whole earth, to show himself strong in the behalf of them whose heart is perfect toward him" (2 Chron. 16:9, KJV). Don't we desire the Lord's eyes to rest on us with favor? After all, eternity is a long time compared to the short days we will spend here on the earth. I believe the Lord is raising up many in these last days who will not compromise.

When you understand that the blessing of the Lord is upon those who walk in integrity, then it becomes easy to remain steadfast and not compromise your heart. David understood this principle, and that is one reason God was able to bless him the way He did in spite of his sins. "But as for me, I will walk in mine integrity: redeem me, and be merciful unto me" (Ps. 26:11, KJV). Oh, how David understood integrity. This is something that needs to be taught again in our churches. It needs to be taught in our homes. The devil has taken these principles out of our schools so they need to be taught even that much more by those of us who, like David, value integrity.

THE SURE MERCIES OF DAVID

I believe this was why the Lord was able to make the covenant with David that He did. It was because of the heart of David. Notice the following scripture concerning King David:

Incline your ear, and come unto me: hear, and your soul shall live; and I will make an everlasting covenant with you, even the sure mercies of David (Is. 55:3, KJV).

**But now thy kingdom shall not continue: the Lord
hath sought him a man after his own heart, and
the Lord hath commanded him to be captain over
his people, because thou hast not kept that which
the Lord commanded thee (1 Sam. 13:14, KJV).**

**And when he had removed him, he raised up unto
them David to be their king; to whom also he gave
testimony, and said, I have found David the son
of Jesse, a man after mine own heart, which shall
fulfil all my will (Acts 13:22).**

Can you see it? God had to judge David when he sinned,
but the Lord said His mercies would never part from the
house of David. This was so because David walked in his
integrity. When he could have taken the quick and easy way
to the throne by slaying King Saul he refused to do so. Even
when he cut off part of Saul's garment the Word tells us his
heart smote him.

Think of it. Most people would have jumped at the opportunity to slay their enemy after being chased all over the
land of Israel as David was. But David allowed the Lord to
promote him. And in the end he came out on top. And so will
you if you also walk in the integrity of your heart. David was
quick to forgive and acknowledge his sin and repent before
God, not from the outward appearance but from the heart.

In the above text in Isaiah 55, the Father God is letting us
know He desires to extend those same mercies to whoever
will come to Him with an open heart. Even in the Old
Testament the Lord made available to the people who would
seek Him the mercies of David.

In Solomon's prayer to God when he was dedicating
the temple, he made mention of the mercies of David. This
proves that all men knew these mercies. They may not have

taken advantage of them, but they were aware of them for they were obvious in the life of David.

> **Now therefore arise, O Lord God, into thy resting place, thou, and the ark of thy strength: let thy priests, O Lord God, be clothed with salvation, and let thy saints rejoice in goodness. O Lord God, turn not away the face of thine anointed: remember the mercies of David thy servant (2 Chron. 6:41-42).**

The minister's life of obedience is a life that will always seek to walk in integrity with the knowledge that, when needed, 1 John 1:9 is available.

> **But if we walk in the light, as he is in the light, we have fellowship one with another, and the blood of Jesus Christ his Son cleanseth us from all sin. If we say that we have no sin, we deceive ourselves, and the truth is not in us.**

> **If we confess our sins, he is faithful and just to forgive us our sins, and to cleanse us from all unrighteousness. If we say that we have not sinned, we make him a liar, and his word is not in us.**

> **My little children, these things write I unto you, that ye sin not. And if any man sin, we have an advocate with the Father, Jesus Christ the righteous (1 John 1:7–2:1).**

To walk in integrity means to be true to one's own heart. And when mistakes are made to be quick to go to the Father and confess those sins and receive forgiveness by faith. It is foremost a life of honesty with oneself and others.

THE TRUTH SHALL SET YOU FREE

Remember what Jesus said about knowing the truth and being set free? I believe here is a great part of walking in integrity—being honest with oneself.

And ye shall know the truth, and the truth shall make you free. They answered him, We be Abraham's seed, and were never in bondage to any man: how sayest thou, Ye shall be made free? Jesus answered them, Verily, verily, I say unto you; whosoever committeth sin is the servant of sin (John 8:32-33).

Notice that the folks who heard Jesus that day refused to know the truth about them. Yes, the Word of God is the truth. But the truth of the Word of God will first illuminate the truth about us so we can then make the changes needed in order to be partakers of His nature. These folks listening to our Lord were not people of integrity for they chose not to believe the truth about themselves.

Integrity says, "I don't want to sin or miss it, but if I do sin I will acknowledge my sin and turn away from it and endeavor to do better by the grace of God." That's what integrity is all about.

Men can see only the outside, but the Lord sees the heart. Man can see only the natural or physical, but the Lord sees the spiritual. He can see and know the very deepest part of our being. The Word tells us:

Neither is there any creature that is not manifest in his sight: but all things are naked and opened unto the eyes of him with whom we have to do (Heb. 4:13, KJV).

As ministers, when we walk in the knowledge of this truth, we will walk in integrity. We will understand it is not important what man thinks about us. It is only important what the Lord thinks about us.

When the praise of man is gone, God sees the heart. When all the work of the day is through, God sees the heart. When the song is sung and the sermon is over, God sees the heart. When we make our long prayers and say amen, God sees the heart. When all is said and done, God sees the heart! Let's purpose in our hearts to be men and women of integrity.

Is there any alternative for us? Can we as ministers afford to be men and women who walk and live in anything less than integrity?

The souls of many thousands of people depend on it. Our churches are depending on it. Our families and friends are depending on it. Our ability to work with trust and confidence with other people depends on it.

The development of the newborn believer depends on it. I remember how disappointed I was the first time I went to a "minister's meeting." What I saw was such lack of honesty and so much work displayed to put on a good face that it almost turned me against the ministry. When I left that meeting I was so disappointed.

But I soon realized that too often ministers put up a front when down on the inside they are hurting. If anyone should be able to be genuine with each other it should be ministers. But, sad to say, that is not the case. Some ministers, however, shine as jewels in honesty and integrity.

And it is seeing these men and women that encourages my heart to know there are still some "Daniels" out there who refuse to be defiled with the compromise of their integrity. When the heart of man is made right with God it becomes a matter of conscience. To obey our heart and conscience is to keep our hearts undefiled by the meat of the world. Even when everyone around us would say, "It's all right to join us in this—everybody is doing it." In these times the righteous man of integrity says, "No. Everyone may be doing it, but that doesn't mean I'm going to do it."

I believe it's a matter of making a decision to do the right thing and then *not* to open the door even the least bit to doing the wrong thing. This, like so many areas in our lives, is something in which all of us can grow. Like Job we can hold on to our integrity with the help of the Lord.

VII.

FOLLOW ME AS I FOLLOW CHRIST

For though ye have ten thousand instructors in Christ, yet have ye not many fathers: for in Christ Jesus I have begotten you through the gospel. Wherefore I beseech you, be ye followers of me.

For this cause have I sent unto you Timotheus, who is my beloved son, and faithful in the Lord, who shall bring you into remembrance of my ways which be in Christ, as I teach every where in every church (1 Cor. 4:15-17).

Be ye followers of me, even as I also am of Christ (1 Cor. 11:1).

To understand the minister's life of obedience is to understand that the minister is to be an example to the world of what Christianity is all about. I like something Martin Luther said in his notes so long ago.

WHY GOD PLACES CHRISTIANS IN THE WORLD

God placed His church in the midst of the world, among countless external activities and callings, not in order that Christians should become monks but so that they may live in fellowship and that our works and the exercises of our faith may become known among men. For human society, as Aristotle said, is not an end in itself but a means [to an end]; and the ultimate end is to teach one another about God. Accordingly Aristotle said that society isn't made by a physician and a physician or by a farmer and a farmer. There are three kinds of life: labor must be engaged in, warfare must be carried on, governing must be done. The state consists of these three. Consequently Plato said that just as oxen aren't governed by oxen and goats by goats, so men aren't governed by men but by heroic persons (August 31, 1538).[9]

Oh, what a responsibility! But it is much more a joy to be in the service of the God of this universe. What a privilege to be called of God to touch people's lives with the gospel of our Lord Jesus Christ. While being the right example to others is a great responsibility, it is also a great joy and opportunity.

For none of us liveth to himself, and no man dieth to himself. For whether we live, we live unto the Lord; and whether we die, we die unto the Lord: whether we live therefore, or die, we are the Lord's (Rom. 14:7-8, KJV).

There is no way to escape the fact that every person on this earth will have an influence on others. It may be either a positive or negative influence, but our lives will affect the people who know us. But the minister, because of God's call to win the peoples of the world, is going to have an even greater influence on others.

That's why it is so important to be the kind of minister who is qualified to be the example people can follow. The apostle Paul was just such a person. Notice again what he said in the above text. He said Timothy would remind the church at Corinth of "my ways, which be in Christ, as I teach everywhere in every church."

In other words Paul's life was an expression of the love of God and the Word of God in such a consistent way that it was the same everywhere he went. He taught the same truths everywhere both by precept and by example.

As you read the writings of Paul it is clear that he taught both the *legal* and the *vital* side of the gospel. In other words he taught 1) who we are in Christ and 2) how to live out in this life who we are in Christ. It is not enough to teach that we should love one another. We must also *live* that love toward one another.

The Word of God gives us those areas in which the minister is to be an example. All of them are important. And ministers must learn obedience in each one of them if they are to be the right kind of example people can follow:

Let no man despise thy youth; but be thou an example of the believers, in word, in conversation, in charity, in spirit, in faith, in purity (1 Tim. 4:12, KJV).

Let's look at this verse a little more closely. Notice the areas Paul told Timothy he was to exemplify. First of all Timothy was to be an example in *word*. That means his speech. In other words Timothy was to see to it that everything that came out of his mouth was wholesome and ministered grace to the hearers.

How very important it is for the minister to learn obedience in the discipline of saying the right thing. Not only must the minister's words *not* be offensive, but they must also be in agreement with the Word of God.

And this is exactly where we all get into trouble more than we would like to admit. More ministries have been damaged and have failed because of the wrong words coming out of the mouth. Every word we speak will have an influence on others. Not just from behind the pulpit either, but when we are outside the church.

What's coming out of our mouths at home, at the supermarket or at the service station getting gas? At the end of the day, if we have not offended someone with our tongues, then we have won a great battle in life.

Now there are times when as ministers we will offend people with the gospel. And that is a different issue. Even Jesus in His ministry offended people with the gospel to the point that on one-occasion multitudes stopped following Him. And all ministers must remember this so discouragement doesn't come when people leave them for the gospel's sake.

Not many of you should become teachers, my brothers and sisters, for you know that we who teach will be judged with greater strictness. For all of us make many mistakes. Anyone who makes no mistakes in speaking is perfect, able to keep the whole body in check with a bridle (James 3:1-2, NRSV).

Here the Word of God makes it plain that the "perfect" man is the one who makes no mistakes in speaking. The power of the tongue cannot be overstated. The tongue can be either a blessing or a cursing. It can create dreams, or it can destroy a lifetime of work.

As ministers we need to remember the power of the tongue. Many books have been written on the power of the tongue, so I will not try to deal with this part of discipleship exhaustively. But a few things must be kept before us on a daily basis as ministers if we are to please the Lord and finish the race He gave us with joy. Now let's notice Proverbs 15 to learn more about the power of the tongue.

A wholesome tongue is a tree of life: but perverseness therein is a breach in the spirit (Prov. 15:4, KJV).

The Hebrew word translated "wholesome" here is *marpe* and has several meanings: curative, medicine, deliverance, cure, healing, remedy, soundness, (Strong's Hebrew Greek Dictionary). In other words our tongues can produce life.

Death and life are in the power of the tongue: and they that love it shall eat the fruit thereof (Prov. 18:21, KJV).

Therefore as ministers we need to be the right kind of example in our speech.

Now let's go back to the second area the minister is to be the right example in, according to Paul's letter to Timothy. He said to be an example in "conversation." Now the word "conversation" here really is talking about behavior. This means the way we carry ourselves and act in all the affairs of life. This is talking about our conduct. Remember that many times our every move is being watched *and* imitated. It's amusing to me how people are such imitators. People do what they see other people do even if it's ridiculous.

Years ago there was a television program called "Candid Camera." You may remember how a cameraperson would hide and film the reactions of people doing the funniest things. Once on the program a man was walking the streets of a crowded city and looking straight up into the air. It was so amusing to watch people pass by and look up into the air to try to find out what this man was looking at. This illustrates the point well that people imitate what they see other people do. Therefore as ministers we should remember that our conduct should be an example for people to follow.

The next thing Paul told Timothy to be an example in was "charity" or love. We know the word translated "charity" really means "love." So as ministers we are to be an example of the love of God. Are we as ministers expressing to a sick and dying world the love of God? Or are we just busying ourselves with selfish desires? Love, or I should say God's love, is something this world needs to see in action. Especially by those who are called by the name of Christ and who have a high calling as ministers. People are looking for such love that is unconditional and does not condemn them. Only the love of God that has been shed abroad in our hearts can meet the needs of a sick, hurting, dying and going-to-hell humanity.

As you may know by now Andrew Murray is one of my favorite ministers of the past. And in one of his sermons he makes the following statements:

To abide in His love, His mighty, saving, keeping, satisfying love, even as He abode in the Father's love—surely the very greatness of our calling teaches us that it never can be a work we have to perform; it must be with us as with Him, the result of the spontaneous out flowing of a life from within, and the mighty in working of the love from above. What we only need is this: to take time and

study the divine image of this life of love set before us in Christ.[10]

To love the unlovable, the unthankful, sometimes ugly and persecuting sinner requires a love that is the result, as Andrew Murray says, "of the spontaneous out flowing of a life from within." All who have been born again and have tasted of the heavenly gift have received the love of God in their hearts. But it is up to each one of us to become obedient to that love and reach beyond ourselves in purpose and grace. To go the extra mile for the sake of those who will one day choose eternal life. That's the example we are called to, and that's the example all ministers must live up to. Rev. Murray states in his sermon "The Fruit of the Spirit Is Love" the following:

The Lord Jesus Christ came down from heaven as the Son of God's love. "God so loved the world that He gave His only begotten Son." God's Son came to show what love is, and He lived a life of love here upon earth in fellowship with His disciples, in compassion over the poor and miserable, in love even to His enemies, and He died the death of love. And when He went to heaven, whom did He send down? It was the Spirit of love, to come and banish selfishness and envy and pride, and bring the love of God into the hearts of men. "The fruit of the Spirit is love."[11]

Need we say more? The entire life of Christ was one of selflessness in a world of selfishness. This is part of the high calling of the ministry, to let the love of Christ be seen in us. We must obey this law of love. We must not fail to do so, for many lives depend on our obedience.

There is no greater reward than to be privileged to look into the eyes of one we just led to Jesus and see the tears of joy roll down his or her face and the newfound glow of God that has just come to live inside that person. What a joy to know that when in heaven we will see people there because of our obedience to the law of Love.

Many are hoping we will not fail. Though they may not know Jesus as their Lord, and though they may persecute us, yet they are hoping we do not fail. They want to believe in a greater love than they have known. For deep within every heart is that desire to be loved by the love of God.

Rev. Murray continues:

And now He calls us to dwell and to walk in love. He demands that though a man hates you, still you love him. True love cannot be conquered by anything in heaven or upon the earth. The more hatred there is, the more love triumphs through it all and shows its true nature. This is the love that Christ commanded His disciples to exercise. What more did He say? "By this shall all men know that ye are my disciples, if ye have love one to another."[12]

This is our duty. This is our responsibility. This indeed is our joy and commission. Moreover this is where our focus should remain by shedding light in a very dark world.

EXAMPLE IN SPIRIT

The apostle Paul continued by telling Timothy to be an example in "spirit." What does this mean? I believe it is talking about meekness of spirit and leadership in personality. Rev. Kenneth E. Hagin once taught us in Bible school that we should be careful of the people we associate with because we pick up the "spirit" of those with whom we spend time.

If a person has a prideful spirit it shows on the outside. If a person has a selfish spirit it shows on the outside. And whatever makes a person ugly on the inside will make that person ugly on the outside.

Have you ever been around someone who irritated you and you didn't know why? Maybe it wasn't anything you could put your finger on so to speak, but you knew you didn't want to be around that person. I believe this is why Paul wanted us to be an example in spirit.

On the other hand have you ever been around people who carried themselves in such a way you admired them and enjoyed being near them? Here is the positive example of a good spirit. A good spirit carries with it all the attributes of the fruit of the spirit. It's amazing, however, that at times the very character that makes a good spirit will sometimes make sinners nervous. But even those same sinners will respect a man or woman of a good spirit.

He that hath knowledge spareth his words: and a man of understanding is of an excellent spirit (Prov. 17:27).

Would to God we were all men and women of an excellent spirit! In the Old Testament, Daniel was such an example of an excellent spirit.

You may recall that in Daniel 5 Belshazzar saw the hand of God write on the wall. It was in a language nobody could read. But the king's advisors recommended that Daniel interpret the writing because of the excellent spirit he had. Notice the following:

There is a man in thy kingdom, in whom is the spirit of the holy gods; and in the days of thy father

light and understanding and wisdom, like the wisdom of the gods, was found in him; whom the king Nebuchadnezzar thy father, the king, I say, thy father, made master of the magicians, astrologers, Chaldeans, and soothsayers; forasmuch as an excellent spirit, and knowledge, and understanding, interpreting of dreams, and showing of hard sentences, and dissolving of doubts, were found in the same Daniel, whom the king named Belteshazzar: now let Daniel be called, and he will show the interpretation (Dan. 5:11-12).

The Hebrew word translated "excellent" actually means "preeminent" (Strong's Hebrew Greek Dictionary). In other words something about Daniel caused him to stand out in the crowd. It made him different from everybody else. And that something was the hand of the Lord that was upon his life.

This is part of what makes a good leader. Even in the natural world, whether in government or the military or in a business, those men and women with excellent spirits are noticed, and they are usually the ones promoted. God is calling the church and ministers especially to be people with an excellent spirit. Notice again the following verse:

Then this Daniel was preferred above the presidents and princes, because an excellent spirit was in him; and the king thought to set him over the whole realm (Dan. 6:3).

This excellent spirit Paul was talking to Timothy about causes some people to be real leaders. An excellent spirited person will not react the same way when a crisis comes.

The crowd will get upset and immediately say, "What are we going to do?" But a person of an excellent spirit will shine in times of trouble.

It seems that nothing bothers these people. The truth is, they are people like all of us, but they have learned to allow the life of God on the inside to dominate them. The leadership qualities of steadfastness and wisdom glow in these people in times of trouble.

Now all of us are gifted differently and have different roles to play in the body of Christ, but nonetheless *all* of us can be men and women of an excellent spirit. It is a matter of choice and of growing up in the Lord. The following scripture bears this out:

My son, forget not my law; but let thine heart keep my commandments: For length of days, and long life, and peace, shall they add to thee.

Let not mercy and truth forsake thee: bind them about thy neck; write them upon the table of thine heart: so shalt thou find favour and good understanding in the sight of God and man (Prov. 3:1-4).

Here is an example of an excellent spirited person who finds favor and good understanding in the sight of God and man. But the above person is not to be one of a select few. This is available to all who will not forget the law or Word of God. Two of the most outstanding attributes of a person with an excellent spirit are in the above verse: mercy and truth. These attributes are the dominant ones in people with excellent spirits. They are merciful to others and honest with themselves and others. Ministers who display such attributes are pillars in the church and examples in the world.

EXAMPLE IN FAITH

Let's look now at the other two areas in which Paul told Timothy to be an example. The next one Paul mentions is *faith.* The minister of the gospel must be a person of faith. Everything about the gospel must be received, understood and known by faith. Indeed, the Word of God tells us:

But without faith it is impossible to please him: for he that cometh to God must believe that he is, and that he is a rewarder of them that diligently seek him (Heb. 11:6)

Now faith is the substance of things hoped for, the evidence of things not seen (Heb. 11:1)

In these verses the Hebrew writer tells us that faith must be a way of life for the believer.

It is one thing to have faith and not exercise it and quite another to be an example in faith. The minister of faith is a leader in stability and steadfastness. While the Bible is full of examples of people of faith, one stands out to me as a leader exemplifying faith: Moses at the Red Sea.

Can you imagine the noise of fear as a million Israelites began to scream and cry when the Egyptian army was closing in on them? With their backs against the Red Sea and nowhere to go they all looked to Moses for leadership. And here is where Moses' faith stood out. In obedience to God he stretched forth his hand over the sea, and the waters parted. Oh, what an example of faith as the children of Israel went over to the other side on dry ground. When fear tried to grip their hearts all they had to do was look at Moses who stood there in faith and believed God.

How the world needs true examples of faith. They are looking for leaders who will inspire them to remain calm in the storms of life. The example of faith is Jesus Christ himself. Remember Paul told the Corinthians to follow him as he followed Christ. A true leader or minister will be a follower of Christ. When we as ministers look to Christ and keep our eyes on Him people will notice. They will think, "If he or she can do it, then I can do it." If a minister is full of fear, people will know it. If a minister trembles on the inside when a storm of life comes, the people will know it.

If a minister steps away and takes the back seat when true leadership is needed, the people will know it and refuse to follow that minister. But if a minister shows leadership by standing with his face into the wind of adversity and refusing to be moved, the people will also recognize it and will follow that minister into the place of victory in Christ.

We know the greater the battle, the darker the night. But when it seems all hope is gone, these are the times when people look for true leaders of faith. They look for leaders who not only speak words of faith but also live a life of faith.

This is the life of obedience. This is the life of faith. This is the life of leadership. This is the life of the minister, being the example that people can follow. Some ministers try to be crowd pleasers. Some ministers depend on their charisma to cause people to follow them, while other ministers look to their education or other talents to promote themselves and cause people to follow them.

But in times of crisis all the education and natural ability and charisma simply slip away and become nothing. In these times people will flee from the self-appointed and self-quali-fied minister and look for a minister whose leadership abilities rest not on his own talents but on Him who created this great universe.

EXAMPLE IN PURITY

Who shall ascend into the hill of the Lord? or who shall stand in his holy place? He that hath clean hands, and a pure heart; who hath not lifted up his soul unto vanity, nor sworn deceitfully. He shall

receive the blessing from the Lord, and righteousness from the God of his salvation (Ps. 24:3-5).

Now we come to another most important area in the minister's life where he should be a good example. It is the area of *purity*. The above text tells us that the individual who desires to go into the presence of the God of this universe must be pure. Accordingly a pure heart is one that does not allow deceit in it.

In other words it is a heart that desires to be open and honest before the Lord. This is the person who will receive blessings and righteousness from the Lord. This is the person who is willing to be corrected by the Lord when he misses it.

The Hebrew word translated "pure" here means empty, clear, clean and pure (Strong's Hebrew Greek Dictionary). In other words purity is a condition of the heart where no contaminants are allowed. It is a heart that allows the Lord to wash it with His Word. It is a heart that is teachable and easy to be entreated. That means it will submit and listen to reason. It is a heart that is compliant with God's Word. Let's examine some other scriptures about purity to gain a greater understanding.

Unto the pure all things are pure: but unto them that are defiled and unbelieving is nothing pure; but even their mind and conscience is defiled (Titus 1:15).

Blessed are the pure in heart: for they shall see God (Matt. 5:8).

Let us draw near with a true heart in full assurance of faith, having our hearts sprinkled from an evil conscience, and our bodies washed with pure water (Heb. 10:22).

We know that conscience is the voice of the human spirit. When we receive Christ into our hearts, we are cleansed from an evil conscience. That's the miracle of the new birth. But from the time we are born again till the time we go home to be with the Lord we must keep our hearts clean from the contaminants of the world. Therefore purity is not an option. It is a requirement for all who would see God. We keep our hearts pure by refusing to allow the entrance of sin or anything that is not pleasing to God.

By compromising a little at a time and letting things into our hearts that should not be there, we are becoming harder and harder on the inside to the point that our hearts no longer condemn us when we sin.

As an illustration of this, one day while attending Rhema Bible Training Center, Rev. Kenneth E. Hagin told us a true story, one he witnessed himself. He told us years ago when he was a boy he used to visit an old man who lived by himself in a small cabin.

This man had a potbelly stove in the middle of his cabin, and he would cook or boil coffee on that stove. Brother Hagin said he would boil that coffee until the old coffeepot just shook on that stove. But the amazing thing was when the old man would drink his coffee; he would gulp it straight down all in one breath. You may find this hard to believe but no more than what we see elsewhere in the world today. Indeed the hardness of this man's body can be a direct parallel to the hardness of the hearts of men.

Kenneth Hagin said he would grab his own throat when he saw the man do that. He would be so amazed when the man did this time and again. But one day the old man told Kenneth how he did it.

"Now, Kenneth," he said, "you might be wondering how I can drink that boiling coffee straight down like that. I didn't start off drinking my coffee that hot. But over the years I kept drinking it hotter and hotter until now I am callused.

My mouth and throat and esophagus are so hardened now that I can't feel it when I drink that boiling coffee."

Rev. Hagin proceeded to tell us Bible students that that is the same way people get hardened on the inside. They don't start off that way, but over the years they allow more and more unclean things in their hearts until they can't feel their consciences. As I said earlier we keep ourselves pure by cleansing ourselves. Remember this verse:

Having therefore these promises, dearly beloved, let us cleanse ourselves from all filthiness of the flesh and spirit, perfecting holiness in the fear of God (2 Cor. 7:1).

We understand that sins of the flesh are those things we can see, such as adultery or murder and so on. But sins of the spirit are those sins that cannot be seen. They are sins of the heart such as unbelief, unforgiveness, jealousy and so on.

These are all areas in which the minister must remain pure so he can be the kind of example the Lord wants him to be. Again this was why the Lord was able to bless David as He did. David kept his heart pure before the Lord.

Can it be done? Yes! Is it always easy? No! But with the help of the Lord and His Word we can do it. We can walk in purity of heart before God and men. And we can thank God there is a continual cleansing by the blood of Jesus for all who walk in the light of the Word of God.

[9]Thomas Nelson Inc., *Heritage of great evangelical teaching: Featuring the best of Martin Luther, John Wesley, Dwight L. Moody, C.H. Spurgeon and others [computer file], electronic ed.,* Logos Library System, (Nashville: Thomas Nelson) 1997, c1996.

[10]Thomas Nelson Inc., *Heritage of great evangelical teaching: Featuring the best of Martin Luther, John Wesley, Dwight L. Moody, C.H. Spurgeon*

and others [computer file], electronic ed., Logos Library System, (Nashville: Thomas Nelson) 1997, c1996.

[11]Thomas Nelson Inc., *Heritage of great evangelical teaching: Featuring the best of Martin Luther, John Wesley, Dwight L. Moody, C.H. Spurgeon and others [computer file], electronic ed., Logos Library System,* (Nashville: Thomas Nelson) 1997, c1996.

[12]Thomas Nelson Inc., *Heritage of great evangelical teaching: Featuring the best of Martin Luther, John Wesley, Dwight L. Moody, C.H. Spurgeon and others [computer file], electronic ed., Logos Library System,* (Nashville: Thomas Nelson) 1997, c1996.

VIII.

PRESSING TOWARD THE MARK

Not as though I had already attained, either were already perfect: but I follow after, if that I may apprehend that for which also I am apprehended of Christ Jesus. Brethren, I count not myself to have apprehended: but this one thing I do, forgetting those things which are behind, and reaching forth unto those things which are before, I press toward the mark for the prize of the high calling of God in Christ Jesus (Phil. 3:12-14, KJV).

One of the most amazing truths in the Word of God is the fact that before the creation of the world, Christ knew each one of us and ordained a plan for our lives. Hidden deep within the heart of the Father God we existed. Our very breath or spirits actually came from the Father Himself.

Here is the miracle of conception. It takes more than just a male and female to produce life; the spirit of life in that embryo comes from God Himself. The part of each one of us that will exist forever is the spirit of man, which comes from God. That's why the Word tells us in Hebrews that God is the Father of spirits.

Furthermore we have had fathers of our flesh, which corrected us, and we gave them reverence: shall we not much rather be in subjection unto the Father of spirits, and live? (Heb. 12:9, KJV).

God is the Father of spirits! That means we all came from God!

That's why the Word of God tells us it is not God's will that any should perish. It is God's will that all come to repentance and receive the heavenly gift and be born again. Everyone will come to the place as a child when he or she will die spiritually. Every baby is alive unto God. But when they reach the age of accountability they will choose death because of the sinful nature of Adam.

And that's exactly why Jesus said, "You must be born again" (John 3:7, KJV). The apostle Paul understood this truth and taught it to the church at Rome.

For I was alive without the law once: but when the commandment came, sin revived, and I died (Rom. 7:9, KJV).

What Paul meant here was that until he had received the knowledge of good and evil, his spirit man was alive unto God. But when he reached the age of knowing good from evil he chose sin and died spiritually.

Now spiritual death is separation from God. That's why men must be born again. But every man must make that choice. And when we do so the life of God becomes part of our spirit and we become the sons of God. We become partakers of the divine nature.

But after we are born again we need to understand that we must continue to choose the life of God. We must desire to follow the purposes God has for each one of us. And that is what Paul is talking about in the above text. He had a revelation of this truth and understood God had so much more for him to walk in.

And he wanted all that God had for him. But wanting it was not enough; he had to *press* into the things of God. He had to press toward the mark for the prize of the high calling. He had to do it. And so must we. Every one of us who will know the purposes God has for us must also press into them.

The reason is simple. Pressing is necessary because the enemy of our souls would hinder us if we let him. The flesh would hinder us if we let it. Other people would hinder us if we let them. Circumstances of life would hinder us if we let them. These are the struggles of life. These are the battles of the believer. This is the fight of faith for the believer, to walk by faith, to live by faith, to refuse to allow anything from stopping us from pressing into all God has for us.

Moreover God's will doesn't happen automatically. We can see this in the world. For people will say, "Why did God allow that to happen?" They say things like that because they don't understand or know the Word of God. They don't understand that because of Adam's sin the devil has a foothold in this world.

So they blame God for every bad thing that happens. But God is not responsible for everything that happens. The devil is doing some things. And people are making choices. And often bad things happen in our lives because we make the wrong choices. Even after we are born again and become Christians, we must continue to make the right choices in life. This is what the apostle Paul meant in our text. He was going to make the right choice for his life.

It was not enough for him to get to heaven. He wanted to achieve all God had for him to achieve in this life. He aspired to finish his race. He desired with all that was in him to be able to hear the Lord say one day, "Well done." He wanted to discover the depths of the grace of God. He was consumed by this desire. Why? Because the Lord put that desire in his heart, just as He did in your heart. Many do not know it or understand it, but that desire is there. For the child of God that desire comes up out of our spirit like wells of water.

The desire to know God's will is in us, but we have to press into it. We must choose to discover the secrets of the plan of God. It's important for all of us who are believers to find and walk in our destiny. But for the minister it is even more imperative to find and walk in God's will. To press is something we must do knowing that if we seek the Lord with all our hearts then He is faithful to show us every step we need to take along life's way.

The Greek word translated "press" in our text is *dioko*, which means to "pursue" (Strong's Hebrew Greek Dictionary). In other words the call of God was the first thing in Paul's life. Paul didn't run after the approval of men. He didn't follow after all the things so many ministers follow after. He had only one goal. And that goal was the most important thing in Paul's life.

Again here is where obedience comes in. Many ministers have failed to walk in their destinies because they pursued the desires of the flesh instead of the will of God. The flesh cries out for power, for pride and for people to serve it. But that's not the kingdom of God. Jesus made that plain to us when He was here on the earth. He said His kingdom "was not of this world" (John 18:36, KJV). Remember what the apostle John said about this world?

For all that is in the world, the lust of the flesh, and the lust of the eyes, and the pride of life, is not of the Father, but is of the world (1 John 2:16, KJV).

These are the things the minister must not follow after if God's will is to be done. And all these things are the tools the devil will use to sidetrack the servants of the Lord. That's why Paul said he had to "press toward the mark" in our text. He wanted to please the Lord more than anything else.

King Saul is an example of a minister who chose to go his own way instead of God's way. And you can see the result of that choice in his life. Though the anointing was upon him to do God's will, he failed by allowing the lusts of the flesh to control him. He allowed his power to go to his head. And it is a sad story indeed to read of the fall of King Saul in the Word of God.

All too often the same thing is apparent in the body of Christ today. Many ministers have fallen because they failed to press toward the mark for the prize. That which God has for each one of us truly is a prize. Nothing in this life could begin to compare with the blessings and joys that lie ahead of us as we pursue God's will.

The apostle Paul earlier in our text made the point that nothing can be compared to the destiny the Father God had for him. Notice what Paul says here:

But what things were gain to me, those I counted loss for Christ. Yea doubtless, and I count all things but loss for the excellency of the knowledge of Christ Jesus my Lord: for whom I have suffered the loss of all things, and do count them but dung, that I may win Christ (Phil. 3:7-8, KJV).

Paul suffered the loss of all things that he may win Christ. In other words he was saying the race he was in was the one the Lord had prepared for him to run. And we must understand that our Lord has a race for each one of us to run also.

Wherefore seeing we also are compassed about with so great a cloud of witnesses, let us lay aside every weight, and the sin which doth so easily beset us, and let us run with patience the race that is set before us (Heb. 12:1, KJV).

Let's consider what the Lord tells us here from His Word.

First of all, the Hebrew writer knows we are in a race. Second, he knows those in heaven are watching us as we run our race. They are cheering us on as if they are saying, "You can do it." "Don't stop now" is the message they are telling us if we could hear them.

I remember years ago while pastoring a small church in Florida the Lord spoke to me and asked me to look up the word "set" in Hebrews 12:1. Let's notice the definition, and then I'll tell you what the Lord said to me about it. According to Strong's Hebrew Greek Dictionary, the word is *"prokeimai, prok'-I-mahee*; from G4253 and G2749; to lie before the view, i.e. (fig.) to be present (to the mind), to stand forth (as an example or reward): —be first, set before (forth)."

Now the idea is that what God has for us was laid out ahead of time. In fact the Word of God bears this out. I'll show some other scriptures along this line later. But let's go back to what the Lord said to me about this verse. The Lord told me three things were set before us.

First, He said we have an appointed *destination*. All of us have an appointed end. That is of course in heaven, to live in the presence of the Lord forever. Even the lost have this destination if they would turn to Jesus and receive Him as

Lord. Second, we have an appointed *path to* that destination. That is our walk here on this earth. And that includes the will of the Lord for us day by day in this life.

Third, the Lord said *revelation* of that path was available to all God's children. He won't reveal to us everything all at once, but His Word and His Spirit will lead us into the perfect will of God.

There is no joy outside the will of God. People will try to find joy elsewhere, but genuine joy comes only from the Lord and submitting to Him. Although the Father God has a path for each of us to walk in, that doesn't mean it will happen automatically. I believe you can understand this by the fact that all too often we made the wrong choices in life.

Millions of men and women are looking for purpose in life. They want something they don't understand, while it is happiness they can't find. That's where we come in as ministers of the gospel of Jesus Christ. We know that what they are looking for comes only by knowing Jesus and walking in His will. As ministers we *must* press into the plan of God; nothing else will do. Now notice the following scriptures along this line:

Remember this, and show yourselves men: bring it again to mind, O ye transgressors. Remember the former things of old: for I am God, and there is none else; I am God, and there is none like me, declaring the end from the beginning, and from ancient times the things that are not yet done, saying, My counsel shall stand, and I will do all my pleasure (Is. 46:9-10, KJV).

Then the word of the LORD came unto me, saying, Before I formed thee in the belly I knew thee; and before thou camest forth out of the womb I sanctified thee, and I ordained thee a

prophet unto the nations. Then said I, Ah, Lord GOD! behold, I cannot speak: for I am a child. But the Lord said unto me, Say not, I am a child: for thou shalt go to all that I shall send thee, and whatsoever I command thee thou shalt speak (Jer. 1:4-7, KJV).

So it is clear from these verses that God has a plan for us and that plan was prepared before the foundation of the world. Now you may say, "That's fine if you are called to be a minister, for Jeremiah was a prophet. But what about me?" The answer is the same for everyone.

According as he hath chosen us in him before the foundation of the world, that we should be holy and without blame before him in love: having predestinated us unto the adoption of children by Jesus Christ to himself, according to the good pleasure of his will (Eph. 1:4-5, KJV).

God has a purpose for each of us, but we must choose the will of God for our lives. We must, as Paul said, press toward the mark. Once we make up our minds and hearts that we will pursue the will of God, then in faith and patience we will see the reality of the hand of the Lord in our lives.

The favor of our Lord will begin to manifest as we take the path He has made ready before us. It is an adventure in faith. It is a way of life. It is a life with purpose and expectations as we walk together with the Lord.

One thing we can do is pray on a daily basis for God's will to be done. "Thy kingdom come, thy will be done, in earth, as it is in heaven" was the prayer of Jesus (Matt. 6:10). The will of God must be prayed out. When we pray for it, when we believe for it, when we expect it to be revealed, it will come to pass.

At times it will amaze us as we look back and see the hand of the Lord upon our lives even when we didn't know it or understand it. But the mighty hand of the Lord is upon those who choose God's will. He makes a way where there is no way. He opens doors for those who desire His will.

THE FAVOR OF THE LORD

When I talk about walking in our destiny, I'm reminded of the fact that all through our lives as believers the favor of the Lord is available to us. Indeed without the favor of the Lord the minister cannot obtain all that God has for his ministry. And without the favor of the Lord ministers are left with formalism, ritualism and the pursuit of natural things in which they try to find success.

So many ministers are empty and unfulfilled because they have either lost the favor of the Lord or they have never really pursued it, for with God's favor come happiness, joy, fulfillment and purpose. And the minister or any believer who has obtained God's favor will exemplify that favor in every area of their lives.

My son, forget not my law; but let thine heart keep my commandments: for length of days, and long life, and peace, shall they add to thee. Let not mercy and truth forsake thee: bind them about thy neck; write them upon the table of thine heart: so shalt thou find favour and good understanding in the sight of God and man (Prov. 3:1-4, KJV).

Here the Lord tells us that if we walk in His Word and walk in truth and forsake not mercy, we would find favor and understanding in the sight of God and man. To press toward the mark is to obtain the favor of God. And when His favor is yours nothing can stop you from fulfilling the plan of God for your life. There is no end to the benefits that can come your way when God's favor is upon you.

The Word of God has several examples of this very truth. Those with God's favor always come out on top. Notice the following scripture:

> **But the Lord was with Joseph, and showed him mercy, and gave him favour in the sight of the keeper of the prison. And the keeper of the prison committed to Joseph's hand all the prisoners that were in the prison; and whatsoever they did there, he was the doer of it. The keeper of the prison looked not to any thing that was under his hand; because the Lord was with him, and that which he did, the Lord made it to prosper (Gen. 39:21-23, KJV).**

Now you remember the story of Joseph. Here's a man who faced more than any of us will ever have to face in life. Think of it! His own brothers sold him to a band of thieves, who when they got to Egypt sold him again, and he became a slave in Potiphar's house.

And while serving there the wife of Potiphar tried to commit adultery with Joseph. In the natural Joseph couldn't win regardless of what he did. But Joseph kept himself pure regardless of what it seemed to cost him. Of course after this he was thrown into prison. Talk about a bad day!

It was a dirty, stinking dungeon with criminals all around. This was what the devil did to Joseph. But because God's hand was upon him and the favor of the Lord was upon him, Joseph would not stay there. Eventually he was brought up out of that prison and was promoted in Egypt to be second only to Pharaoh.

This is what the favor of God will do. It may appear as if everything is going wrong, but if we keep our hearts right in the sight of God He will promote us and cause us to find favor with man. When you are walking in the favor of the Lord, nothing can stop you. When the entire world is pushing you down, the Lord will be lifting you up. Indeed if God be for us, who can be against us? No man can stop the favor of our God!

Another example of the favor of the Lord is found in the story of Esther. Her life is a story of the purposes of God coming to pass not only for her but also in the lives of the remnant of the Jews who lived in Persia.

And the king loved Esther above all the women, and she obtained grace and favour in his sight more than all the virgins; so that he set the royal crown upon her head, and made her queen instead of Vashti (Esth. 2:17, KJV).

All through the book of Esther it is written that she obtained favor in everything she did. Why? Because God's hand was upon her and gave her that favor so the purposes of God would come about. We know in reading her story that the Lord had her in the right place at the right time to save the Jewish people from certain destruction.

Oh, how wonderful to see the favor of the Lord upon our lives. To realize and understand that as His children if we keep our hearts right and walk in the light of His Word then His favor will be upon us. That favor will be given to us in the sight of men for the purpose of God to be realized in our lives. Daniel was another example of the favor of the Lord. Over and over again the Lord gave him favor in every situation in which he found himself.

Now God had brought Daniel into favor and tender love with the prince of the eunuchs (Dan. 1:9, KJV).

Every time the devil tried to destroy Daniel God brought him out on top because of His favor. Daniel never compromised his faith. And though it looked as if it would cost him, in the end it was the very thing that brought him out on top.

For thou, Lord, wilt bless the righteous; with favor wilt thou compass him as with a shield (Ps. 5:12, KJV).

Never underestimate the favor of the Lord; it covers us as a shield. That means it protects us when others try to harm us. The more the devil tries to hinder us, the more the favor of God protects and delivers us.

Years ago while on a mission trip to Alaska the Lord showed me something about prosperity that He wanted me to share with the Native Americans there. As I was studying Joshua 1:8 I learned something about the word "prosper."

This book of the law shall not depart out of thy mouth; but thou shalt meditate therein day and night, that thou mayest observe to do according to all that is written therein: for then thou shalt make thy way prosperous, and then thou shalt have good success (Josh. 1:8, KJV).

I found that the word "prosperous" here comes from the Hebrew word *tsalach*, which means, "to push forward and break out" (Strong's Hebrew Greek Dictionary). In other words God prospers us by causing us to push forward and break out of all that would hold us back.

Many of God's people including ministers are so intimidated that they refuse to take any steps forward if doing so would rock the boat. Moreover, many fail to understand that it is during times of adversity and challenges that the purposes of God can come to pass. At times the Lord has to move us into that place where His will can be done. Even when others oppose us we can press toward that mark of the high calling of God in Christ Jesus. The more they oppose us, the more God promotes us. This is the favor of the Lord.

IX.

RESTING IN THE ANOINTING

The Spirit of the Lord is upon me, because he hath anointed me to preach the gospel to the poor; he hath sent me to heal the brokenhearted, to preach deliverance to the captives, and recovering of sight to the blind, to set at liberty them that are bruised, to preach the acceptable year of the Lord (Luke 4:18, KJV).

There can be no life of obedience by the minister or any believer without understanding something about the anointing and how to rest in that anointing. Without a genuine knowledge of this subject the minister is at a great disadvantage. Instead of learning to lean upon the power and strength of the Lord in times of trouble, those who fail to understand the anointing and how to rest in it will find themselves depending on their own strength and thus failing.

But the Lord doesn't call anyone to the ministry to fail. Failure has no place in the life of the believer or the minister. We touched a little on this earlier in this book, but now I want to address the anointing and how to rest in it in more detail.

THE NECESSITY OF BEING ANOINTED

In the above text we learn several things. First of all we learn that our Lord and Savior had to be anointed to do the works He did. Jesus did not do one single miracle or good work until after the Father God anointed Him in the Jordan River. As we learned earlier Jesus had to be anointed because when He came to the earth He stripped Himself of all His power and privileges. He had to depend on the anointing or power of the Holy Spirit to do everything He did. Indeed it was the Father God Himself who performed all the works of Jesus Christ on the earth.

And so must we. God has anointed us as He has Jesus. And this anointing will enable us to do the same works Jesus did when He was here on the earth.

Verily, verily, I say unto you, He that believeth on me, the works that I do shall he do also; and greater works than these shall he do; because I go unto my Father (John 14:12, KJV).

The anointing is what enables us to do these same works Jesus did. If Jesus could not do any works without the anointing, neither can we. But praise God we have been anointed. We have been called and anointed by the same Holy Spirit.

But to better understand what this anointing is let us determine what the anointing is not.

The anointing is not natural ability or talent or the measure of one's education. The anointing is something that comes from God and draws attention to God, not to man. It is the power of God.

How God anointed Jesus of Nazareth with the Holy Ghost and with power: who went about doing good, and healing all that were oppressed of the devil; for God was with him (Acts 10:38, KJV).

Notice in the above verse that Jesus was anointed with the Holy Ghost and with power. So the anointing is the manifested presence of the Holy Spirit and His power. I like to say it this way: The anointing is the power of God in you and upon you to enable you to do what you could not do in yourself.

When the children of Israel rebelled against God and refused to go into the Promised Land it was because they forgot the power of the anointing and what it could do. They refused to enter into the rest of God because they had such a lack of understanding about the anointing.

And that's exactly why every minister and every believer must understand the anointing so they can enter into the rest of God. Resting in the anointing is resting in the love of God and the power of God, knowing the greater one will put us over for He is with us.

It's not the will of the Lord that ministers live in turmoil and fear. It is not the will of the Lord for the minister to be dominated by people and what they think should be done. And yet so many ministers live this way. They have given into all sort of fears and failed to enter in to the rest of God because they either didn't understand the anointing or didn't pursue it.

How I've learned over the years to depend upon the anointing. What a joy to know the power of God is resting upon me. Even when I don't feel it or perceive its presence, I know it is there. But as all of us must do, I must exercise faith in that anointing, thus casting all my care upon the Lord and entering into His rest.

Come unto me, all ye that labour and are heavy laden, and I will give you rest. Take my yoke upon you, and learn of me; for I am meek and lowly in heart: and ye shall find rest unto your souls (Matt. 11:28-29, KJV).

For we which have believed do enter into rest, as he said, As I have sworn in my wrath, if they shall enter into my rest: although the works were finished from the foundation of the world (Heb. 4:3, KJV).

This is the will of God for each of us who is a believer—to have rest. But we cannot have this rest until we believe what the Lord has done for us. And thank God He has anointed us. Oh, how that anointing will transform us. It will change us from being fearful and running from our enemies to having faith and courage and running toward our enemies so we may lie hold on all that belongs to us in Christ.

The anointing will lift us up above our weaknesses. It will cause us to come out of our little caves where we have hidden ourselves for fear that someone will see us. It will free us from the fear of man and grant to us great boldness to stand up for the Lord and become obedient to Him. This is part of the minister's life of obedience.

By being more aware of the presence of the anointing than we are of other things around us we can rest and be in perfect peace even in the middle of life's greatest battles. We can learn to trust the anointing, for it will not fail us. The anointing that every child of God has will guide and teach us everything concerning the work of God in our lives. But we must make the decision to listen to and obey that anointing.

But ye have an unction from the Holy One, and ye know all things. But the anointing which ye have

**received of him abideth in you, and ye need not
that any man teach you: but as the same anointing
teacheth you of all things, and is truth, and is no
lie, and even as it hath taught you, ye shall abide
in him (1 John 2:20, 27, KJV).**

According to the above verses, that anointing will teach
us all things. And we can depend on everything that anointing
teaches us, for He is the Spirit of truth. This is why we can
rest in the anointing; we can be assured He will never fail.
There is no anointing apart from the presence of the Holy
Spirit, for the anointing and the Holy Spirit are one and are
equivalent. So we must listen to Him and depend on Him,
for He will never fail.

When David stood up to the giant Goliath he did so
without fear because he had experienced the power of the
anointing. He knew the same anointing that helped him kill
the lion and the bear would also help him kill the giant. As
ministers and indeed simply as believers we are called to live
the same kind of life, a life without fear because we know we
have been anointed.

Oh, how that anointing has not been altered. It is full of
power. It radiates with life-giving power to heal. It consists
of all that is part of the Holy Spirit Himself. It is our shield,
our source, our strength and our ability. Why should we be
afraid?

When David killed that giant he did so by the anointing.
When the children of Israel crossed the Red Sea they did so
by the anointing. When Samson pulled down the walls of the
enemy of the Jews he did so by the anointing. When Samson
used the jawbone of an ass to kill hundreds of soldiers, he
did so by the anointing.

When the waters of the Red Sea were parted the anointing
parted them. When the walls of Jericho fell they did so by the
anointing. All throughout history the anointing of the God of

this universe has done what no man could do. That's what we are to have faith in. That's why we can rest, for the same power of God that did all those miracles so long ago lives on the inside of each and every one of us.

THE PROGRESSIVE WORK OF THE ANOINTING

Every minister must comprehend, however, that the anointing is measurable. And we must know the work of the anointing in our lives is a progressive work. We can see this so clearly in the Word of God. Understanding this progressive work of the anointing will help us rest because we will realize we can have more of His power when we need it. Notice the following verses that will illustrate this point:

> **I will sprinkle clean water upon you, and you shall be clean from all your uncleanness, and from all your idols I will cleanse you. A new heart I will give you, and a new spirit I will put within you; and I will remove from your body the heart of stone and give you a heart of flesh. I will put my spirit within you, and make you follow my statutes and be careful to observe my ordinances (Ezek. 36:25-27, NRSV).**

Can you catch a glimpse of the progression of the work of God in our lives? First, God says He will sprinkle clean water upon us. Second, He says He will put a new heart in us, one that is soft and full of His nature. Third, He says He will then put His Spirit within the one changed.

When we as ministers understand this progressive work of the anointing in our lives, we can rest because we will know God is not finished with us yet. That's what Paul meant when he said, "I count not myself to have apprehended" (Phil. 3:13, KJV).

Paul knew a supply of the Spirit was available to him that would be exactly what he needed at the hour. When he trusted God and His Word that supply of the Spirit would manifest. And when it did so, circumstances would change. Darkness would then turn to light. The power of God and the glory of God would break forth upon the scene.

For I know that this shall turn to my salvation through your prayer, and the supply of the Spirit of Jesus Christ, according to my earnest expectation and my hope, that in nothing I shall be ashamed, but that with all boldness, as always, so now also Christ shall be magnified in my body, whether it be by life, or by death (Phil. 1:19, KJV).

This was why Paul could rest when he was in prison. He had seen and known the power of God. From the very beginning of his experience with God he saw the anointing in manifestation. We may not have had the exact experiences the apostle Paul had in the anointing, but all of us have experienced it in the new birth and the infilling of the Holy Spirit.

We can rest because we have the same anointing living in us that raised Jesus from the dead. It's the same anointing that allowed Jesus to walk on the water and empowered Him to heal the sick and raise the dead. We can rest in that anointing. We can live in that anointing. Indeed we can be consumed in that very anointing as it provides for us each day the power of God.

BREAKING THE YOKE BECAUSE OF THE ANOINTING

And it shall come to pass in that day, that his burden shall be taken away from off thy shoulder, and his yoke from off thy neck, and the yoke shall

be destroyed because of the anointing (Is. 10:27, KJV).

Here we observe that the anointing will destroy or, as we say, break the yoke. Too often ministers wear the wrong kind of yoke. Instead of wearing the Lord's yoke that He said was easy and light, many ministers wear the yoke of bondage. Hence the reason many ministers are powerless to help others in the Body of Christ. Bondage can come in many shapes and sizes. At times ministers have allowed the traditions and teachings of men to take the place of the Word of God. And the apostle Paul called this a yoke of bondage.

Stand fast therefore in the liberty wherewith Christ hath made us free, and be not entangled again with the yoke of bondage (Gal. 5:1, KJV).

In Paul's day the yoke of bondage was the law. Many of the Jews wanted to make keep it a requirement for salvation. Today we spot the same thing in different forms. But if the minister is bound up in various kinds of bondage, then how can he minister liberty to others when ours is a gospel of liberty that sets men free? Religion will always bind people with a yoke of bondage, but the gospel is a gospel of liberty!

So, too, ministers as well as believers need to be free in order to free others who need it. When one looks at the world today millions of people have never heard about the anointing. But it is up to us to tell them. We must allow the anointing to free us, and then we can move out and set the captives free by that same anointing.

The same power of God that healed in Jesus' day is available to heal in our day. We must combine faith with the anointing in order for it to work for us. The power of God and His anointing will never manifest where people are saturated with doubt and unbelief.

How can the minister be used of the Lord to set others free if he or she is bound up with the wrong yoke? In Jesus' day the carpenters had to be master craftsmen. When a man wanted to buy a yoke for his oxen he couldn't go down to 84 Lumber and pick one out. Instead he would go to a carpenter who would make the yoke to fit his oxen.

So the carpenter worked on that yoke until it was right. If the yoke did not fit the animals properly, then blisters would wear away on the animals hindering them from being able to work. That's why what Jesus says about His yoke is so revealing.

> **Take my yoke upon you, and learn of me; for I am meek and lowly in heart: and ye shall find rest unto your souls. For my yoke is easy, and my burden is light (Matt. 11:29-30, KJV).**

The meaning of the word "easy" in this verse carries the idea of being well fitting. Notice what Vine's Expository Dictionary says about this word:

> *chrestos* (5543) primarily signifies "fit for use, able to be used" (akin to *chraomai*, "to use"), hence, "good, virtuous, mild, pleasant" (in contrast to what is hard, harsh, sharp, bitter).[13]

Therefore the yoke Jesus is talking about is the perfect plan of God that is well fitting to the individual and will not work for another. When we understand this truth and that it is the anointing that carves out God's will for us and makes it fit for service, we can rest. We can be at perfect peace and rest in who we are in Christ.

Each and every one of us as ministers have our own individual part to play in the building up of the kingdom of God on the earth. We can rest in that. We can rest in God's plan. We can recognize that as individuals it's all right to be different as long as we are serving the Lord with all our hearts.

When we understand this truth, the spirit of competition will go out the door and the spirit of cooperation will come in the door. As a fine-tuned watch every piece will fit in place and work by doing its part. The world will no longer see the one but the whole body of Christ acting in unison so the will of the Lord will be done upon the earth.

We can rest in who we are in Christ. And there will be no need for recognition from man but only that recognition that comes from the Lord. We will rest in the yoke the Lord has for us, and wearing that yoke will become easy. It will not be a hard thing to do, rather it will be the natural thing to do. This is part of the rest our Father God has for us all if we will walk in it.

Our completeness and fulfillment rests in Him. Our joy and sense of success rests in Him. Our total well being—spirit, soul and body—rests in Him and in believing that what the Father has for us is the best thing for us. We can rest in the anointing. The Lord will never let us down. All fear flees away as we rest in His anointing. Indeed the attacks of the enemy flee away as we rest in the anointing.

---

[13]W.E. Vine, Merrill F. Unger and William White, *Vine's complete expository dictionary of Old and New Testament words [computer file], electronic ed., Logos Library System*, (Nashville: Thomas Nelson) 1997, c1996.

X.

SEALED BY
THE HOLY SPIRIT

Now he which stablisheth us with you in Christ,
and hath anointed us, is God; who hath also
sealed us, and given the earnest of the Spirit in
our hearts (2 Cor. 1:21-22).

W e can rest in the anointing for the anointing also has
sealed us. What a wonderful and comforting thought
to know all the things our Father has done for us. When we
have obtained a revelation of the above scripture we can have
confidence in who we are in Christ. What then is this sealing
by the Holy Spirit? First, let's look at the Greek meaning of
the above words and go on from there. The following is a
definition of the word "sealed."

sphragizo, sfrag-id'-zo; from G4973; to stamp
(with a signet or private mark) for security or
preservation (lit. or fig.); by impl. to keep secret,

to attest:—(set a, set to) seal up (Strong's Hebrew Greek Dictionary).

To be sealed therefore means to stamp with a signet or private mark. The obvious reference here is that in days gone by kings possessed a special signet they used to stamp anything whose authenticity they wanted to show. Anything stamped thus was secure and preserved as being the property of the king. So this stamp of the king would represent three things: 1) ownership, 2) authenticity and 3) protection. Since the Holy Spirit also has sealed us we can claim these three things. Because of this seal we must know we belong to the Lord. We must also know we are new creatures in Christ. And we must recognize that we are under His protection because of this seal by the Holy Spirit.

Moreover this sealing is something that is in the past tense; it is an accomplished fact. We are not going to be sealed, for the Holy Spirit already seals us.

All these things are so important for us to remember, but it is especially imperative for the minister to remember them; the work the Lord has for the minister demands it. Without an inclusive knowledge of these truths the minister is at a complete disadvantage. Notice what Nelson's New Illustrated Bible Dictionary says about this signet.

SIGNET — a seal or ring used by an official much like a personal signature to give authority to a document. The Old Testament indicates several uses of the ring seal.

Pharaoh gave his ring to Joseph (Gen. 41:42) as a badge of his delegated authority. Ahasuerus gave his ring to the wicked Haman (Esth. 3:10, 12) then gave it to Mordecai after Haman's treachery was exposed (Esth. 8:2). King Darius of Persia

sealed the lion's den after Daniel was placed in it (Dan. 6:17).

The signet was an emblem of royal authority (Gen. 41:42). Zerubbabel, who had been chosen by God to lead the returned captives in Jerusalem (Hag. 2:23), was compared to a signet ring, signifying that God had invested him with the highest honor.[14]

Notice again that we have been sealed by the Holy Spirit, meaning the Holy Spirit is the guarantee deposit of the fulfillment of the promise of our inheritance. We belong to the Lord. We are authorized by the Lord. We are protected by the Lord. We know that no man can pluck us out of the Father's strong hand.

No test can move us away from the blessed hope that we will be glorified. No power of darkness can defeat us or stop for one minute the mercies of the Lord from flowing into our lives. All because of Jesus and His sacrifice the Holy Spirit has sealed us.

This truth that our God has sealed us should bring great joy to our hearts!

Let's further notice the definition of the word "seal."

SEAL — a device such as a signet ring or cylinder, engraved with the owner's name, a design, or both (Ex. 28:11; Esth. 8:8). A medallion or ring used as a seal featured a raised or recessed signature or symbol so it could be impressed on wax, moist clay or ink to leave its mark (Job 38:14).

The seal was strung on a cord and hung around the neck or worn on one's finger (Gen. 38:18, NRSV; signet ring, Jer. 22:24). A seal usually served to certify a signature or authenticate a letter or other document (Neh. 9:38; Esth. 8:8; John 3:33).

In the New Testament, Pilate authorized a guard to be sent to secure the tomb where the body of Jesus had been laid: "So they went and made the tomb secure, sealing the stone and setting the guard" (Matt. 27:66).

The word "seal" is used also in a figurative sense of an outward condition (John 6:27; 1 Cor. 9:2; 2 Tim. 2:19). The Book of Revelation uses the word frequently in this sense (Rev. 5:1; 7:2-8).[15]

Likewise the Lord has put his stamp upon us as upon soft clay, according to the Word of God in the book of Ezekiel.

A new heart also will I give you, and a new spirit will I put within you: and I will take away the stony heart out of your flesh, and I will give you an heart of flesh. And I will put my spirit within you, and cause you to walk in my statutes, and ye shall keep my judgments, and do them (Ezek. 36:26, 27, KJV).

We have been stamped with the signet of the King. We are God's property. We are authorized to go forth and do the work of the ministry in His name. This sets us apart from the traditions and customs of religion. The Lord in the Word of God reminds me of two very significant examples of this sealing.

One takes place during the instance of Ezekiel the prophet. In order to understand properly the significance of the example in Ezekiel we must first understand the background of the writings of Ezekiel. His writings and ministry take place during the time of Nebuchadnezzar, king of Babylon, who destroyed Jerusalem in three stages. Let's notice the following from "Talk Thru the Bible":

Nebuchadnezzar destroyed Jerusalem in three stages. First, in 605 B.C., he overcame Jehoiakim and carried off key hostages including Daniel and his friends. Second, in 597 B.C., the rebellion of Jehoiakim and Jehoiachin brought further punishment; and Nebuchadnezzar made Jerusalem submit a second time. He carried off ten thousand hostages including Jehoiachin and Ezekiel. Third, in 586 B.C., Nebuchadnezzar destroyed the city after a long siege.[16]

Before the third and final stage of the destruction of Jerusalem the Lord had the prophet Ezekiel to prophesy over the city. Now what takes place here is quite interesting in light of the seal of God upon us today.

In Ezekiel 9 the Lord told the angels of judgment not to bring judgment until the righteous remnant were sealed. All else was to be destroyed. But those who had the seal of God upon their foreheads were spared and protected. We will notice that the judgment of God was to begin at the sanctuary of God.

This tells us of the great responsibility of the ministers of the Lord to be obedient to all the Lord tells them, for they are watching for the souls of men. And because of this truth, judgment always begins at the house of God. Now let's notice Ezekiel 9.

He cried also in mine ears with a loud voice, saying, Cause them that have charge over the city to draw near, even every man with his destroying weapon in his hand. And, behold, six men came from the way of the higher gate, which lieth toward the north, and every man a slaughter weapon in his hand; and one man among them was clothed with

linen, with a writer's inkhorn by his side: and they went in, and stood beside the brazen altar.

And the glory of the God of Israel was gone up from the cherub, whereupon he was, to the threshold of the house. And he called to the man clothed with linen, which had the writer's inkhorn by his side; and the Lord said unto him, Go through the midst of the city, through the midst of Jerusalem, and set a mark upon the foreheads of the men that sigh and that cry for all the abominations that be done in the midst thereof.

And to the others he said in mine hearing, Go ye after him through the city, and smite: let not your eye spare, neither have ye pity: Slay utterly old and young, both maids, and little children, and women: but come not near any man upon whom is the mark; and begin at my sanctuary. Then they began at the ancient men which were before the house (Ezek. 9:1-6, KJV).

Can you perceive here the significance of the seal of God that was upon their foreheads? Oh, how this should help our faith. If we can comprehend the fact that we likewise have the seal of God upon us, we would face life fearlessly. How much more can those of us who have the call of God to the ministry have confidence to obey the Lord in the work He has given us to do?

Nothing can stop us because we are sealed. Nothing can harm us because we are sealed. We may not be able to see that seal, but the devil and his cohorts can see it. The angel of the Lord sees it. And that's all who need to see it. We can rest in the fact that it is there. We are God's property. God has authorized us. God has anointed us.

All the Father God has is at our disposal to use for His work upon the earth. Can anything beat that? I think not! This blessed truth should mean so much more to us the closer we get to the end of the ages. We know we are living now in the last days. The church age is rapidly coming to a close. Prophecies are being fulfilled so rapidly that it's difficult to keep up with them. While it may look dark in the world, yet we know that now is the greatest time for harvest the world has ever known.

Unparalleled opportunities abound for the minister of the gospel today. We have all the modern technology available to us that has sent men to the moon. And while the devil is using this technology for his purposes, yet we know this knowledge has come from the Lord to spread the gospel to a sick and dying world.

The other example of this sealing by the Lord is found in the book of Revelation. And of course it takes place during the tribulation upon the earth known as the great tribulation period. Let's notice now the following passage:

And the fifth angel sounded, and I saw a star fall from heaven unto the earth: and to him was given the key of the bottomless pit. And he opened the bottomless pit; and there arose a smoke out of the pit, as the smoke of a great furnace; and the sun and the air were darkened by reason of the smoke of the pit.

And there came out of the smoke locusts upon the earth: and unto them was given power, as the scorpions of the earth have power. And it was commanded them that they should not hurt the grass of the earth, neither any green thing, neither any tree; but only those men which have not the seal of God in their foreheads (Rev. 9:1-4, KJV).

During the darkest period of judgment that will come upon the earth, the protection of God will rest on those who have been sealed by God. I find it interesting that both cases of protection are in the ninth chapters of Ezekiel and Revelation. As ministers we don't need man's approval or authorization, for the Holy Spirit has sealed us. The ability we will need to obey and do the work of the Lord is ours, for the Holy Spirit has sealed us. No government agent who is possessed by the devil can stop us, for the Holy Spirit has sealed us.

In crossing the greatest seas the minister need not fear, for the Holy Spirit has sealed us. While flying in the skies to foreign lands we need not be afraid, for the Holy Spirit has sealed us.

Oh, how the books of heaven will show us one day just how many thousands of times the God of this universe has provided for His own who have been sealed by the Holy Spirit.

As I travel and minister to different churches, I often tell the congregations I believe there will be a library in heaven. Of course I make it plain I have no scripture on it to back up this opinion, so I could be wrong. But it's my conviction that when we get to heaven we will be able to see the many times the Lord had His hand upon us and protected us from danger and even death.

I believe each and every event is recorded in heaven for us to look at one day to the glory of God. If I'm wrong, then so be it. But the truth remains that we will be judged out of the books of heaven, so therefore the Lord does keep good records. But once we understand that the Holy Spirit has sealed us life becomes much easier.

We can then walk by faith with a greater measure of confidence and joy. We will be able to rest in our individual callings and gifts. We won't need to look on the outside for help because we know the greater one resides on the inside.

And that greater one will provide for us. That greater one will protect us. That greater one will use us to the glory of

God. So remember as you obey the Lord that the Holy Spirit has sealed you. If indeed the Holy Spirit has sealed us who are believers, then we should live our lives accordingly.

We should never forget we are God's property and belong to Him. And if we remember this precious truth we will be less inclined to live our lives as we will. Instead we will endeavor to live our lives in submission to His will. We will find it easier to obey the Word of God and the Spirit of God.

There will be no more room in our thought processes to say, "This is my ministry." Indeed since we belong to the Lord, then everything we have also belongs to the Lord. We will understand more fully that we are simply stewards of the things of God. And as stewards we will give an account one day of our stewardship.

Moreover by remembering this truth we will live in a greater measure of peace with our fellow believer, for we will remember they are God's property as well. We will be careful to take better care of God's property. As pastors we will remember church members are not our people but property of the Father God.

Our homes will be more peaceful if the husband and wife both remember their mate is the property of the Father God. We will be careful how we treat God's property and thereby have a greater respect for one another. I recall once in my own life how the Lord reminded me that my wife was His daughter and that I would do well to take care how I treat God's daughter. Therefore we would all do well to remember that the Holy Spirit seals us.

---

[14]Ronald F. Youngblood, general editor; F.F. Bruce and R.K. Harrison, consulting editors, *Nelson's new illustrated Bible dictionary: An authoritative one-volume reference work on the Bible with full color illustrations [computer file]*, electronic edition of the revised edition of *Nelson's*

illustrated Bible dictionary, Logos Library System, (Nashville: Thomas Nelson) 1997, c1995.

[15]Ronald F. Youngblood, general editor; F.F. Bruce and R.K. Harrison, consulting editors, *Nelson's new illustrated Bible dictionary: An authoritative one-volume reference work on the Bible with full color illustrations [computer file], electronic edition of the revised edition of Nelson's illustrated Bible dictionary, Logos Library System,* (Nashville: Thomas Nelson) 1997, c1995.

[16]Bruce Wilkinson and Kenneth Boa, *Talk thru the Bible [computer file], electronic ed., Logos Library System,* (Nashville: Thomas Nelson) 1997, c1983.

XI.

UNDERSTANDING YOUR SPHERE OF INFLUENCE

John answered and said, A man can receive nothing, except it be given him from heaven (John 3:27, KJV).

N ow we come to that component of the minister's life of obedience that very few ministers have understood. It is an essential element of the minister's life. I call it the minister's sphere of influence. John the Baptist made the above statement when someone noticed that Jesus' disciples were also baptizing and that "all men come to Him" (John 3:26, KJV).

In other words a spirit of competition tried to rise up between John's disciples and the followers of Jesus. But John was making it clear that if the people were coming to Jesus it had to be given to Him by God. It was the call of God on Jesus and the purpose of God in His life that caused the people to be drawn to Him.

If only ministers could get a good understanding of this it would eliminate the spirit of competition among different ministries in the body of Christ. But instead all too often ministers forget that the kingdom they are supposed to be promoting is the kingdom of God and not their own little kingdom.

It is so obvious at times that there is such jealousy and envy among ministers. It seems one minister is always trying to outdo another one. Don't misunderstand me. A lot of good ministers in the body of Christ have unselfish hearts and portray the love of God to the world and to their fellow ministers. With that being said, however, there are all too many in the ministry today who have forgotten why they are in the ministry in the first place. It is not our ministry anyway, for it is His work upon the earth.

Instead of being jealous or envious when we see other ministers blessed, we should be thankful. We should rejoice that the Lord is blessing them. We should rejoice when other ministries reach people we may not be reaching.

This is what John was trying to teach his disciples. Now some ministers have appalling attitudes that need to be changed before they can rejoice at the success of other ministries. Some have good hearts, but when they see the success of other ministers the devil tries to tell them they are not doing anything worthwhile for the Lord.

The devil will scream at their minds that they must not be called of God since they aren't doing what other ministers are doing. But all of us, regardless of who we are, need to be reminded of what John told his disciples. We need to understand we can be content with our own calling and equipping. We don't have to look at other ministers and covet their gifts.

God has gifted each and every one of us in the body of Christ in diverse ways. And in the final analysis all praise and credit must go to God, because we are simply laboring with Him in His work. It is not our work anyway. It is the Lord's work. Forget that and you will busy yourself with trying to make things happen the way you think they should.

And then when they don't happen you get frustrated and down on yourself. You listen to the devil as he rubs it in and tears you down. So here is where we need some good biblical knowledge about our individual callings from God. We need to know what we are called to do and learn to leave other ministers alone. We should not judge them or talk negatively about them in any way. We should learn to be faithful with what we are called to do.

We should ask ourselves, "How can I fulfill all that I'm called to do?" And one way we do this is by getting our eyes off other ministers and on the Lord. Remember that if we are faithful God will promote us.

Now it is certain that none of us as ministers can accomplish any more than what the Lord has ordained for us. He must bless us and promote our ministries for His glory. If we maintain the right heart and attitude, the Lord will use us; if not, He won't. But we must also search for the Lord's will for our ministries and pray that all He has for us will come to pass.

With prayer the Lord will begin to use us in what I call our sphere of influence. What is this sphere of influence? It is that circle or boundary we have been given to touch people's lives with for the gospel. Further, God has given that circle to us. Without the Lord we would have no influence at all. He opens doors of opportunity for us. Let's notice some other scriptures along this line to help us get a better view of what I'm talking about here:

For he whom God hath sent speaketh the words of God: for God giveth not the Spirit by measure unto him (John 3:34, KJV).

As we can see from this scripture, the Holy Spirit was not given to Jesus by measure. This implies that we have been given the Spirit by measure. Jesus said Himself that it was not He but the Father in Him who did all the works.

So everything Jesus did was done by the power of the Holy Spirit. The same is true with us as ministers today. The only difference is that we have been given the Spirit by measure. Now, after Pentecost, the Holy Spirit is distributed among the entire body of Christ.

> **How shall we escape, if we neglect so great salvation; which at the first began to be spoken by the Lord, and was confirmed unto us by them that heard him; God also bearing them witness, both with signs and wonders, and with divers miracles, and gifts of the Holy Ghost, according to his own will? (Heb. 2:3-4).**

Now the Greek word translated "gifts" here are *merismos* and means "distributions" (Strong's Hebrew Greek Dictionary). The inference here is that the Holy Spirit has been distributed now to the body of Christ. Now that doesn't insinuate that we can't continue to drink of the water of life. Indeed it is the will of the Father that we continue to desire and receive more of Him through the power of the Holy Spirit.

Now the anointing of the Holy Spirit upon our ministries is the power and equipping that gives us the ability to reach others. Whatever He has called us to do will be the sphere of influence we will have for the gospel's sake.

Now that sphere of influence can grow and become larger if we are faithful with what we have been given now. If we as ministers have not given ourselves to be obedient to what God has called us to do, we can't expect God to give us more to do. Remember this scripture?

> **And I was afraid, and went and hid thy talent in the earth: lo, there thou hast that is thine. His lord**

answered and said unto him, Thou wicked and slothful servant, thou knewest that I reap where I sowed not, and gather where I have not strowed: thou oughtest therefore to have put my money to the exchangers, and then at my coming I should have received mine own with usury. Take therefore the talent from him, and give it unto him which hath ten talents. For unto every one that hath shall be given, and he shall have abundance: but from him that hath not shall be taken away even that which he hath (Matt. 25:25-28, KJV).

So we can see that the principle of faithfulness has much to do with what our sphere of influence is in the work of the Lord upon the earth. Every minister must be faithful with what the Lord has given him to do and not be desirous or envious of the ministry of someone else. Each of us will be responsible and accountable for our own gifting and not the gifting of others.

Now let's notice another passage of Scripture that will shed some light here. As we do, you will notice that the same problem existed in the apostle Paul's day. Many ministers were comparing themselves with other ministers instead of comparing themselves with the Word of God.

For we dare not make ourselves of the number, or compare ourselves with some that commend themselves: but they measuring themselves by themselves, and comparing themselves among themselves, are not wise (2 Cor. 10:12, KJV).

But the apostle Paul makes it clear in this next verse what a tremendous mistake that is.

> **But we will not boast of things without our measure, but according to the measure of the rule which God hath distributed to us, a measure to reach even unto you (2 Cor. 10:13, KJV).**

Paul said that his boasting would not be outside his measure. In other words Paul didn't try to do something outside the sphere of influence God had given him. Notice he said that the Corinthian's were inside the measure or sphere of influence that was given to him by God.

The apostle Paul recognized this measure that was given to him, and he was faithful to continue within the boundaries of that measure. He had no desire to go outside this boundary of ministry. But he understood the Lord could increase that measure or boundary if He so desired. The word translated "rule" here actually means "boundary" in the original Greek (Strong's Hebrew Greek Dictionary).

Now some ministers will actually attempt to go beyond their boundary of influence by "stretching." This is why many are not content to remain within the sphere of ministry God has given them. It's one thing to desire to do more for the Lord and to reach more souls for Him. But it is an entirely different thing to wish for more because of pride or because of being envious of another man's ministry.

> **For we stretch not ourselves beyond our measure, as though we reached not unto you: for we are come as far as to you also in preaching the gospel of Christ: not boasting of things without our measure, that is, of other men's labours; but having hope, when your faith is increased, that we shall be enlarged by you according to our rule abundantly, to preach the gospel in the regions beyond you, and not to boast in another man's line of things made ready to our hand. But he that**

glorieth, let him glory in the Lord. For not he that commendeth himself is approved, but whom the Lord commendeth (2 Cor. 10:14-18).

Can you distinguish the heartbeat of the apostle Paul here? How I wish all ministers would get an understanding of this principle. I believe that if we could it would change our ministries for the better. Many more people would be influenced in this world by the gospel. I also believe sinners would actually see the difference in the attitudes of ministers.

While it is true that many sinners will never accept the Lord regardless of what we may do, it is also true that many of them are looking for more integrity from ministers along this line. I believe the world can see the spirit of competition and jealousy among the churches and among the ministry. But that is where the Lord has given us as ministers the opportunity to be the right kind of examples.

Success in the ministry is not measured by the Lord the same way we measure success. All too often we measure success by the numbers of people we minister to or by the size of our churches. We tend to look on the outward appearance of things. But the Lord looks on the heart.

But what determines your measure of influence? I believe it is the condition of the heart more than anything else. Without maintaining the fruit of the Spirit in our lives we will get lifted up in pride when the Lord uses us. And that kind of attitude will keep us from going on to the next level of ministry.

I believe the fruit of the Spirit must increase at the same pace as the increase of the anointing upon us. If not, one will not walk in the love of God and will thereby yield to wrong spirits. I remember years ago the Lord helped me see He was watching over and guiding my ministry even when I didn't realize it. He also taught me not to go my own way; if I did, it would be hard.

I was feeling dissatisfied with what I was doing for the Lord and didn't understand the Lord had more for me to do. I decided to go for a drive just to get out of the house. As I was driving I heard the Lord speak to my heart and say to me, "Go home and look at Psalm 32:8-9, for I have a word for you."

How excited I was to think that God would speak to me in such a specific way. I immediately turned my car around and headed for home with much expectation. I couldn't wait to find these scriptures to see what the Lord wanted to say to me. It seemed the closer I got to home the more intense the excitement was on the inside of me. Nothing could have been more supernatural to me; I knew I had heard from the Lord. As I got home I couldn't wait to run and get my Bible. I walked into my study and found my Bible and turned it to the passage.

I will instruct thee and teach thee in the way which thou shalt go: I will guide thee with mine eye (Ps. 32:8, KJV).

With tears rolling down my eyes I was so touched and blessed by the presence of the Lord. I was so overwhelmed with emotion to think that the Lord would visit me in such a real way. I remember thanking Him and praising Him for this word when He spoke to me again. This time He said, "I said to look at verses 8 *and* 9."

Then I realized I hadn't even gotten to verse 9 yet! I was so overcome with emotions that I had to take off my glasses and wipe the tears from my eyes so I could continue to read. As I began reading verse 9 I thought, "Did I hear the Lord right?" I continued to think, "What does this mean?"

Be ye not as the horse, or as the mule, which have no understanding: whose mouth must be held in with bit and bridle, lest they come near unto thee (Ps. 32:9, KJV).

As I thought on what this verse meant I could again hear the Lord speak to my heart and tell me, "Son, don't make me force you to do what I've called you to do." Then I saw it. I understood then that I had much to do with whether the will of the Lord was being done in my life.

I'm the one who had to choose to obey Him. And to obey Him meant to walk in the measure of ministry that the Lord had for *me* and not someone else. The Lord continued to tell me, "Don't make me put a bit in your mouth to force you to go where I want you to." I remember saying in tears, "Yes, Lord, I will obey you."

The next thing He told me was He wanted me to go back to Bible school. I had graduated two years prior to this, but now the Bible school I attended was offering another year to their program. The Lord spoke to me in August, and by September I had moved again from Morgantown, West Virginia, to Broken Arrow, Oklahoma.

And what a year I had again at Bible school. It was a good year filled with so much learning about the pastoral ministry. It was God's will for me. It was the sphere in which the Lord wanted me to walk.

Sometimes we as ministers get caught up in the trivial things of life. We are not unlike others in that regard. We have to put our flesh under and refuse to allow it to dominate us. We also have the same emotions that will try to influence us. Because we are called to the ministry doesn't mean we are super human beings with no emotions.

But we must learn to deal with those emotions in order to keep ourselves in a position to be used by God. The minister can look out in front of him or her and realize the sky is the limit, for there is no limit with God. He is not interested in holding us back. He desires for us to excel and reach more people for Him. But we must learn to rest in the timing of the Lord and the will of the Lord.

He cannot, however, advance our ministry faster than we can handle it. We must allow Him to mold us and prepare us for what He has for us to do. As ministers we must learn to be patient and wait on the Lord. We must study to show ourselves approved unto God. We must allow Him to train us.

Then after being trained we can be used by Him. He can only use us to the extent that we are ready. Therefore walk in your measure. Walk in your sphere of influence. Learn to be faithful where you are. As a good soldier of Jesus Christ don't complain when you see others blessed, but rejoice with them.

Don't stand back and say, "Why does he have such a large church?" Don't even think about it. Keep your own heart right with God. Don't fall into the trap of comparing yourself with other ministers. Don't be covetous or envious of their sphere of influence and ministry. Remember that the greater the measure or sphere of influence given to you by God, the greater the accountability we must face.

Not many of you should become teachers, my brothers and sisters, for you know that we who teach will be judged with greater strictness (James 3:1, NRSV).

Not many (of you) should become teachers (self-constituted censors and reprovers of others), my brethren, for you know that we (teachers) will be judged by a higher standard and with greater severity (than other people): thus we assume the greater accountability and the more condemnation (James 3:1, Amp).

It is a sober thing to be called by God into the ministry. Many young ministers only look at the glamour of being seen by people. They look at the ministry from the outward appearance. But the ministry is not a game. Yes, it is a great honor to be called to stand in one or more of the five-fold ministry gifts, but it is also a great responsibility.

If we as ministers understood that, we would be content to say, "Lord, just let me be a doorkeeper in the house of the Lord." Often those ministers with smaller ministries look at larger ministries and wish they could be their ministries. On the other hand those with larger ministries look at those with smaller ministries and wish they could be theirs; they now understand the tremendous responsibility that goes along with it.

Let's allow the Lord to work in us and through us in the measure He has given us and then rest in that measure. Rest in the sphere of influence given to you. It's always easy to look at the grass on the other side of the fence and desire it. But once you get there you may find it was better where you were. Remember what the Lord taught His disciples along this line?

> **Then came to him the mother of Zebedee's children with her sons, worshipping him, and desiring a certain thing of him. And he said unto her, What wilt thou? She saith unto him, Grant that these my two sons may sit, the one on thy right hand, and the other on the left, in thy kingdom. But Jesus answered and said, Ye know not what ye ask. Are ye able to drink of the cup that I shall drink of, and to be baptized with the baptism that I am baptized with? They said unto him, We are able. And he saith unto them, Ye shall drink indeed of my cup, and be baptized with the baptism that I am baptized with: but to sit on my right hand, and on my left, is not mine to give, but it shall be given to them for whom it is prepared of my Father (Matt. 20:20-23, KJV).**

Notice Jesus said to them, "You know not what you ask." In other words you don't know all that is involved with what you ask. It has been said that we should be cautious about what we ask for because we may get it. And so it is in ministry. We need to be sure we understand the responsibility of what we ask of the Lord.

Are we willing to pay the price others have paid to reach the place of ministry where they are? Are we willing to sacrifice and spend the time they spent in prayer to hear from the Lord? Understand that we can only see the result or finished product. But we don't see the preparation and the sacrifices that many have made to be where they are today in ministry.

The Bible has an example about this very thing. We touched on it earlier, but it bears repeating here. And that is the story of Elijah and Elisha. Elisha wanted a double portion of the Spirit that was upon Elijah. And as you know he had to pay the price to receive it.

He had to stay his eyes on the prophet of God. He had to refuse to allow anything to deter him from watching Elijah. And along the way he had every opportunity to fail. But because of his faithfulness and obedience and determination he received what he desired of God. And you can see the result of that in his ministry. It is true that the prophet Elisha had twice the number of miracles in his ministry than Elijah had.

The question is, "Are we willing to pay the same price?" Understand that when we are walking in our own sphere of ministry or influence, the grace of God will rest upon us. If we step out of our place of ministry, the grace of God will be frustrated. But Paul said he did not frustrate the grace of God.

I do not frustrate the grace of God (Gal. 2:21, KJV).

We then, as workers together with him, beseech you also that ye receive not the grace of God in vain (2 Cor. 6:1, KJV).

148

According to the grace of God which is given unto me, as a wise masterbuilder, I have laid the foundation, and another buildeth thereon. But let every man take heed how he buildeth thereupon (1 Cor. 3:10, KJV).

But by the grace of God I am what I am: and his grace which was bestowed upon me was not in vain; but I labored more abundantly than they all: yet not I, but the grace of God which was with me (1 Cor. 15:10, KJV).

Can you see that whatever we do in ministry must be done in the grace of God? None of us can do anything without His grace. It is His ministry. It is His grace. It is His work upon the earth that He has called us to enter into. We are laborers with Christ. It is His work! As ministers we should say, "Here am I, Lord. Use me for your glory," and "It doesn't matter what you want me to do; just help me to be faithful."

To better understand our sphere of ministry or influence for the Lord, we need to understand that all of us are gifted differently. This truth is so evident in the Word of God as one notices the many different individuals who were used by God. We need to understand that often the Lord chooses the least likely candidates in the natural.

For ye see your calling, brethren, how that not many wise men after the flesh, not many mighty, not many noble, are called (1 Cor. 1:26, KJV).

But God hath chosen the foolish things of the world to confound the wise; and God hath chosen the weak things of the world to confound the things which are mighty; and base things of the

**world, and things which are despised, hath God
chosen, yea, and things which are not, to bring to
nought things that are (1 Cor. 1:27-28, KJV).**

**That no flesh should glory in his presence (1 Cor.
1:29, KJV).**

When we look at some people who are used by God we
marvel and wonder how they could ever be used like that.
And when we ask such questions it is clear the Lord has to
get all the glory.

I recall a true story Kenneth E. Hagin shared with us in
Bible school. He was visiting a certain church as an evangelist and was in the church praying when someone came
to seek advice from the pastor. The pastor didn't know he
was in a room next to his praying. When the church member
asked the pastor his question, Rev. Hagin could hear it even
though he didn't try to; as close as he was, he couldn't help
but hear. When he heard the question he wondered how the
pastor would answer it. But when the pastor answered the
church member's question, Rev. Hagin could only cry and
give God the praise. He knew the answer came from God,
not from the pastor.

Kenneth Hagin shared that with us to illustrate that the
least likely people to be used by God are usually the very
ones God uses. Maybe you've seen the same thing in your
lifetime. I know I have. Ministers come in all shapes and
sizes from all kinds of backgrounds, but they are still used
by God. The apostle Paul said:

**For I am the least of the apostles, that am not meet
to be called an apostle, because I persecuted the
church of God. But by the grace of God I am what
I am: and his grace which was bestowed upon me
was not in vain; but I laboured more abundantly**

**than they all: yet not I, but the grace of God which
was with me (1 Cor. 15:9-10, KJV).**

When I look at the diversity of the ministry gifts in the
body of Christ I simply marvel. I'm amazed to notice the
way men and women are used of God. Notice Paul said he
labored more abundantly than them all, but he said it was not
he but the grace of God with him. And we can do the same
thing. We also can minister according to the grace of God
that is with us, remembering the grace of God also refers to
the many gifts given to us to do what He has asked us to do.

**Having then gifts differing according to the grace
that is given to us, whether prophecy, let us prophesy
according to the proportion of faith; or ministry,
let us wait on our ministering: or he that teacheth,
on teaching; or he that exhorteth, on exhortation:
he that giveth, let him do it with simplicity; he that
ruleth, with diligence; he that showeth mercy, with
cheerfulness (Rom. 12:6-8, KJV).**

I also believe it is imperative to keep in mind that we must
walk in our sphere of influence by faith. Our proportion of
faith has much to do with the degree in which we obey the
Lord in our sphere of influence. It will always require faith to
do what the Lord has for us to do. Ours is a full-time job to
stay focused on our own sphere of influence and walk it out
by faith knowing in which our very steps are ordered of the
Lord.

XII.

THE VALUE OF GODLY
RELATIONSHIPS

Behold, how good and how pleasant it is for brethren to dwell together in unity! It is like the precious ointment upon the head, that ran down upon the beard, even Aaron's beard: that went down to the skirts of his garments; as the dew of Hermon, and as the dew that descended upon the mountains of Zion: for there the Lord commanded the blessing, even life for evermore (Ps. 133:1-3, KJV).

I've frequently made the statement while ministering in churches that tomorrow's greatest friend could be your greatest enemy today. This may sound a little extreme, but the principle remains. Many times it is the people we least think will help us as ministers who are the ones that do.

I recall something the Lord said to me a number of years ago. He said, "By following after the law of love, doors of divine appointment will open up to you." What a powerful and true statement that is. To ask ourselves what love would do in all our relationships is to be Christ-like.

The truth of the matter is that we need each other as ministers. We may not think we do but we do. We need to recognize that because we are all gifted differently we need the gifts that are in others. As Paul reminded us, we are members of the same body of Christ upon the earth.

As it is, there are many members, yet one body. The eye cannot say to the hand, "I have no need of you," nor again the head to the feet, "I have no need of you" (1 Cor. 12:20-21, NRSV).

On the contrary, the members of the body that seem to be weaker are indispensable, and those members of the body that we think less honorable we clothe with greater honor, and our less respectable members are treated with greater respect (1 Cor. 12:22-23, NRSV).

In other words we certainly do need each other. There is no such thing in the body of Christ as one member who is more necessary than another member. We all have our part to play. All of us must function in the body as the Lord has placed us there. We must esteem in higher value other ministers rather than ourselves.

Will Rogers once said, "Numbers don't mean anything . . .because it's people that counts" (Maxwell, 10). And so people do count. For the minister of the gospel there is no greater key to success than to comprehend that people count. It's not our programs that count. It's not our wisdom or ability to speak that counts. It's not what our last name is or where we come from that counts.

It's all about people. People are why Christ came to this sinful earth in the first place. Aren't you glad you are one of those people Christ died for? Because the ministry is all about people we as ministers must learn the value of godly relationships. In fact, ignorance in this area will eventually cost us our ministries.

If we cut someone else down we are really cutting ourselves down. There is no escaping this truth. Yet many ministers don't realize this. They live their lives oblivious to other people and their needs, even though they are called to serve others. They see other people as getting in their way to success.

Such narrow thinking is a direct reflection of a narrow walk with the Lord. No one can fail to love men and yet walk with the Lord. We exist as ministers for the people of the world. Our Lord tells us in His Word to "go ye into all the world, and preach the gospel to every creature" (Mark 16:15). People are what we are after.

When ministers fail to see and understand the worth of another person, they are not only limiting the Lord from blessing that person but may also be cutting off a tremendous blessing for themselves. The Lord may use the next person you bless to bless you one day.

That of course is not the reason we minister to other people. We minister to them out of a servant's heart of love. But we should recognize that the Lord puts us into contact with other people at times to help us get the job done. We just can't escape the fact that the Lord will use other people even when we don't think so.

Ralph Waldo Emerson once said, "It is one of the most beautiful compensations of this life that no man can sincerely try to help another without helping himself" (Maxwell, 37). To respect the other person is to respect oneself. To see the worth of another person is to unleash the gifts and talents in that person.

Developing the best in another so as to enable them to reach thousands is better than trying to reach the thousands yourself and failing. As ministers we must remember that we are called to build people up not tear them down. Do you remember the following scripture?

And he gave some, apostles; and some, prophets; and some, evangelists; and some, pastors and teachers; for the perfecting of the saints, for the work of the ministry, for the edifying of the body of Christ (Eph. 4:11-12).

Notice the purpose for ministry is to "edify" the body of Christ. To edify is to build up. Many people will not permit you to help them. They do not want help of any kind, much less from a minister. I've been in numerous situations where it was evident a person I was trying to help simply wanted me to go away.

But other times people responded and gave their hearts to the Lord. So we never know who will receive us or who will not. Maybe the person we are trying to help will end up persecuting us the most. But even in those times the Lord will bring someone our way who will be a great source of encouragement.

The early church knew something about appreciating one another and seeing in one another the value the Lord could see in them. Hence we discover one of the reasons the Lord was able to bless them so much. It released the power of God in their midst. Great signs and wonders were done to the glory of God. And thousands were saved because of that power and love manifested through the people.

RELATIONSHIP OF THE BRETHREN

And they continued steadfastly in the apostles' doctrine and fellowship, and in breaking of bread,

and in prayers. And fear came upon every soul: and many wonders and signs were done by the apostles. And all that believed were together, and had all things common (Acts 2:42-44).

We can learn from the above text that the early church had all things common. That means no one had a superior attitude. Those members of the early church valued their relationships with one another. And that value was a direct reflection of the love they had for the Lord.

This value of others was the result also of the Holy Spirit that was poured out on the day of Pentecost. When the Holy Spirit is allowed to move, as He will among the people, love and unity will be manifested. Such love and respect for one another are so far removed from the world that sinners must stand up and take notice. In the days of the early church, society in general had a greater dependency on the working together of people in a village or neighborhood. And that dependency reflected itself in a more meaningful relationship.

In today's society, however, we discover there is so much more independence—so much in fact that we don't have to depend on our next-door neighbor for anything. Such lifestyles have lent themselves to maintaining our distance from one another even in the church. The result is a lack of concern and mutual respect for each other. We have been so blinded to the fact that we need each other.

Ours is a materialistic society rather than a personal one. So we must labor that much more in the church to develop godly relationships. I use the word *godly* because those relationships ordained by the Lord will be the most meaningful and lasting and mutually beneficial. All of us will need the help of others one day. Notice how the following scripture bears this out.

Two are better than one; because they have a good reward for their labour. For if they fall, the one will lift up his fellow: but woe to him that is alone when he falleth; for he hath not another to help him up. Again, if two lie together, then they have heat: but how can one be warm alone? And if one prevail against him, two shall withstand him; and a threefold cord is not quickly broken (Eccl. 4:9-12).

What powerful truth! Notice that if two work together they have a good reward for their labor. And with this profound truth so evident before us many believers, including ministers, refuse to allow others to help them. It is also evident they need to swallow their pride and admit to themselves and to others that they are people too. In this last hour of the church we need each other even more than ever before.

Remember this verse of scripture? "Iron sharpens iron, and one person sharpens the wits of another" (Prov.27:17, NRSV). This shows us just how much we help each other. It is part of the plan of the Lord for His children to grow and develop with the help of other people. The members of the early church had no problem understanding this.

The power of the Holy Spirit on the day of Pentecost united the disciples as never before. With boldness they proclaimed the gospel. Working together was not a problem then. But it wasn't long until this unity was tested. During the persecution their unity was strong but as the church began to rest from persecution other priorities developed.

A spirit of competition got into the church. And you can see that in the writings of the apostle Paul. As he obeyed the call of God on his life the spirit of jealousy caused great problems in the church. And so it is today. But the status quo is not acceptable. We must avoid this spirit of competition so we can move on to the greater blessings the Lord has for each one of us.

> **For ye are yet carnal: for whereas there is among you envying, and strife, and divisions, are ye not carnal, and walk as men? For while one saith, I am of Paul; and another, I am of Apollos; are ye not carnal? Who then is Paul, and who is Apollos, but ministers by whom ye believed, even as the Lord gave to every man? I have planted, Apollos watered; but God gave the increase. So then neither is he that planteth any thing, neither he that watereth; but God that giveth the increase (1 Cor. 3:3-7).**

So the lesson of placing value on godly relationships was something that had to be learned in the first century church along with every generation since then. As in every generation some never get it, but others understand this truth and go on to become the leaders of their time. Charles Finney in his sermon "Hindrances to Revival" makes the following statements:

> **A revival may be expected to cease when Christians lose the spirit of brotherly love. Jesus Christ will not continue with people in a revival any longer than they continue in the exercise of brotherly love. When Christians are in the spirit of a revival, they feel this love, and then you will hear them call each other brother and sister, very affectionately.**[17]

From Charles Finney's statements I believe it is apparent that when the spirit of revival ceases our love for one another does also. When the church is engulfed in the Holy Spirit and His love it carries out the law of Christ. And that law of Christ is the law of love.

> **Bear ye one another's burdens, and so fulfil the law of Christ. For if a man think himself to be something, when he is nothing, he deceiveth himself. But let every man prove his own work, and then shall he have rejoicing in himself alone, and not in another. For every man shall bear his own burden (Gal. 6:2-5).**

When a man thinks of himself more highly than he should, however, other people become devalued in his eyes. When the verse tells us to bear one another's burdens, it means a heavy weight or large burden. But when the verse tells us every man should bear his own burden, it means a small load or task.

In other words we must all be busy to obey what God has called us to do. But sometimes along the road of life we need someone to encourage us and agree with us in faith. The nature of the devil is selfishness. It says I don't need anyone else. That is what caused the devil to fall in the first place. He focused on himself, so others became devalued, even to the point that he tried to overthrow God. Selfishness breeds contempt for other people because selfishness comes out of a heart of pride that says, "I don't need anyone else; their needs are not important."

> **For I say, through the grace given unto me, to every man that is among you, not to think of himself more highly than he ought to think; but to think soberly, according as God hath dealt to every man the measure of faith (Rom. 12:3).**

According to the above verse it takes faith to let go of the pride of life and see the things in ourselves that God has placed in us and so much the more when it comes to other people. But I can tell you from my own experience in life that I would not even be alive were it not for the help of other people.

As ministers we have the responsibility of being the right kind of example in valuing other people. I remember something taught us in Bible school along this line. Rev. Kenneth E. Hagin told us always to put something into people because too often others are busy taking something out.

So it is our jobs to put something into people, not take something out. In other words don't tear other people down but rather build them up. We must place value in our relationships with others. Jesus placed value in His relationship with us.

VALUING OTHERS

To see the value in others is to see the hand of the Lord at work. It is to realize the wonderful variety in the handiwork of God. To know that the Lord has gifted each and every person for a purpose is to place great value on a person's worth. The Word of God is full of examples of our Lord bringing people together for the promotion of God's plan in their lives.

An example of this is found in the story of Jonathan and David in the Old Testament. Jonathan recognized the value of David; he saw the hand of the Lord upon him. As a result the Lord was able to use Jonathan on a number of occasions to deliver David from his father's envy and wicked plans.

And it came to pass, when he had made an end of speaking unto Saul, that the soul of Jonathan was knit with the soul of David, and Jonathan loved him as his own soul. And Saul took him that day, and would let him go no more home to his father's house. Then Jonathan and David made

a covenant, because he loved him as his own soul. And Jonathan stripped himself of the robe that was upon him, and gave it to David, and his garments, even to his sword, and to his bow, and to his girdle. And David went out whithersoever Saul sent him, and behaved himself wisely: and Saul set him over the men of war, and he was accepted in the sight of all the people, and also in the sight of Saul's servants (1 Sam. 18:1-5).

Jonathan was able to see the worth in David and was willing even at his own expense to help David. He laid down his rights and became the love of God in action. And David recognized the divine appointment with Jonathan and gladly received his help.

As ministers we especially should value our relationships with others, beginning with our relationship with the Father God, to our relationships with our spouses and including our relationships with members of the body of Christ. Along the pathway of life the Lord will bring into our lives certain people who will be faithful friends just as He did with Jonathan and David.

The Lord give mercy unto the house of Onesiphorus; for he oft refreshed me, and was not ashamed of my chain: but, when he was in Rome, he sought me out very diligently, and found me. The Lord grant unto him that he may find mercy of the Lord in that day: and in how many things he ministered unto me at Ephesus, thou knowest very well (2 Tim. 1:16).

The Lord will always bring people into our lives just when we need them to help us in time of trouble. Yes, the Lord is with us. His presence is with us always even to the end of the world.

But the Lord also understands that at times we need to see flesh and blood. We need to be able to hug another person and at times cry on their shoulder. We need to be able to comfort one another with the comfort we ourselves have received of God. We should understand that the help of other people expresses the favor of the Lord to us often. To realize the value of another person means that at times we will be on both the giving and the receiving ends.

Oh, what a joy to give to others, to build them up and encourage them to reach their full potential. To watch the character of Jesus develop in other people is a great reward in itself.

The faces of hurting people turned into joy because we could see the value in them is the most fulfilling experience we could have outside our walk with the Lord. Likewise it is a joy to see the Lord bring another person our way to help us.

We must learn to value our relationships. To value our leaders is to value Christ. To value one another as church members is to value Christ. To value our spouses is to value Christ. To value our children is to value Christ. To do so is to value the gifts and abilities within people.

Inside each of us is a vast storehouse of undiscovered resources placed there by our Lord for building up His body. To value others is to rise above the narrow tunnel vision of self-sufficiency. It opens the door of limitless possibilities as we walk with the Lord.

To allow the anointing to flow upon us in every area of our lives opens the storehouse of heaven. Indeed it is to know Him more.

---

[17]Thomas Nelson Inc., *Heritage of great evangelical teaching: Featuring the best of Martin Luther, John Wesley, Dwight L. Moody, C.H. Spurgeon and others [computer file], electronic ed., Logos Library System,* (Nashville: Thomas Nelson) 1997, c1996.

XIII.

COURAGE UNDER FIRE

Have not I commanded thee? Be strong and of a good courage; be not afraid, neither be thou dismayed: for the Lord thy God is with thee whithersoever thou goest (Josh. 1:9).

And David said to Solomon his son, Be strong and of good courage, and do it: fear not, nor be dismayed: for the Lord God, even my God, will be with thee; he will not fail thee, nor forsake thee, until thou hast finished all the work for the service of the house of the Lord (1 Chron. 28:20).

There can be no discussion of the minister's life of obedi-ence without also discussing the need for the minister to be courageous. I don't believe I have ever met another true minister of the gospel who at least once in his or her life wished the Lord had called someone else. Most ministers understand that, although they wouldn't do anything else in life, they would not have chosen the ministry.

Something of Moses no doubt lies in each of us who have been called as ministers because we have felt or maybe thought, "Lord, send someone else." But in responding to the call of God we have had to submit ourselves and become willing to do what the Lord ordained for us. Only young, naive candidates for ministry would feel they could do a better job than someone else. Therefore the true servant of the Lord has become willing and obedient.

If ye be willing and obedient, ye shall eat the good of the land (Is. 1:19).

Let's look at the definition of courage and get a better understanding of what it is.

Nelson's New Illustrated Bible Dictionary defines courage as:

COURAGE—the strength of purpose that enables one to withstand fear or difficulty. Physical courage is based on moral courage—a reliance on the presence and power of God and a commitment to His commandments (Josh. 1:6-7, 9, 18; 23:6; 2 Chron. 19:11).[18]

Strength of purpose is indeed the ability to go on when difficulty arises. It comes out of a total reliance on the presence and power of God. It is the willingness to obey the Lord in the face of great opposition, knowing He is with us.

The pressures of life come to all of us. I remember a statement Rev. Kenneth E. Hagin would make in Bible school. He would tell us "the pressures of life come to all of us, for we are not immune to them." And so it is. All of us must fight the good fight of faith. Every believer will face persecution and testing.

But the minister will at times face the greatest of challenges. The devil knows if he can stop him or her, then he will hurt many more people at the same time. Many in the body of Christ are looking for leadership. And I'm talking about true leadership that will remain steady under fire. I'm talking about the leadership qualities that were exemplified in David as he faced the giant Goliath. When fear gripped the hearts of the rest of the army the Lord needed someone of faith who could dare trust Him and be used by Him to bring the victory. This is true leadership.

COURAGE COMES FROM THE LORD

Martin Luther in his sermon on Psalm 23 makes the following statement:

Though my temptations were even more numerous and great, and though my lot were even worse, and though I were already in the jaws of death, yet I will fear no evil. Not that I could assist myself through my own care, efforts, work, or help. Nor do I depend on my own wisdom, piety, royal power, or riches. Here all human help, counsel, comfort, and power are far too weak. This, however, avails for me, that the Lord is with me.[19]

He says, "All human help, counsel, comfort, and power are far too weak . . .however . . .the Lord is with me." And even though it is true that at times the Lord uses people to encourage us, in the end the Lord alone is our source and our strength.

At my first answer no man stood with me, but all men forsook me: I pray God that it may not be laid to their charge. Notwithstanding the Lord

**stood with me, and strengthened me; that by me
the preaching might be fully known, and that all
the Gentiles might hear: and I was delivered out
of the mouth of the lion (2 Tim. 4:16-17).**

Of all the examples in the Word of God of ministers
having courage under fire the apostle Paul stands out. The
above scripture clearly reveals what was common in his
ministry rather than the exception. When I think of the kinds
of persecutions and oppositions Paul faced, our little problems, as ministers are nothing by comparison. The saying
goes, "I used to complain that I had no shoes till I saw a man
who had no feet."

Often we complain when really our lives as ministers
today are soft compared to those of the men and women in
days gone by who suffered so much. Of course I'm speaking
primarily of ministers here in the West. In other lands, especially in the Far East and Middle East, ministers must face
much more difficult persecution.

But all of us can take courage from the Word of God
and the power of the Holy Spirit regardless of who we are
or where we may be serving the Lord. We face the same
tests and trials of life. One may be stronger in one area than
another, but all of us will come to the place where we must
learn to depend on the Lord.

We can rest in the fact that the greater the test or trial we
face, the greater the grace of God is ours to confront it. We
must learn to rest in that grace; it is the ability to stand when
everything in our flesh says to run and give up and quit.

**There hath no temptation taken you but such
as is common to man: but God is faithful, who
will not suffer you to be tempted above that ye
are able; but will with the temptation also make**

a way to escape, that ye may be able to bear it (1 Cor. 10:13).

We must also remember that if we listen before a great trial of faith the Holy Spirit will prepare us by filling us with His power, boldness and strength. This is exactly what the Lord did for Joshua. He faced not only Jericho and the battles in Canaan, but he also faced the reality of being the leader in place of Moses.

But over and over again the Lord showed Himself strong on his behalf. Just prior to the crossing of the Jordan River and the battle of Jericho the Lord Himself appeared to Joshua to bless him and give him the courage he needed to face what lay ahead. Do you remember the following scripture? If you receive it, the Lord is saying the same to you today.

And it came to pass, when Joshua was by Jericho, that he lifted up his eyes and looked, and, behold, there stood a man over against him with his sword drawn in his hand: and Joshua went unto him, and said unto him, Art thou for us, or for our adversaries? And he said, Nay; but as captain of the host of the Lord am I now come. And Joshua fell on his face to the earth, and did worship, and said unto him, What saith my lord unto his servant? And the captain of the Lord's host said unto Joshua, Loose thy shoe from off thy foot; for the place whereon thou standest is holy. And Joshua did so (Josh. 5:13-15).

Of course this appearance was the Lord Himself, for an angel would not have permitted Joshua to worship him. While we may not have such visions of Jesus or an angel, yet the presence of the Lord will give us grace before and during the battles of life. Martin Luther continues in his sermon on Psalm 23 by saying:

Thy rod and Thy staff, they comfort me

"The Lord," he says, "is with me, but not bodily so that I might see or hear Him. This presence of the Lord of which I am speaking is not to be grasped by the five senses. But faith sees it and believes surely that the Lord is nearer to us than we are to ourselves." How? Through His Word. He says therefore, "Thy rod and Thy staff, they comfort me." It is as though he would say, "In all of my anxieties and troubles I find nothing on earth that might help to satisfy me. But then God's Word is my rod and my staff. To that Word I will cling, and by it I raise myself up again. I will also learn for sure that the Lord is with me and that He not only strengthens and comforts me with this same Word in all distresses and temptations, but that He also redeems me from all my enemies, contrary to the will of the devil and the world."[20]

As ministers we can take courage under fire knowing that like Paul we are sharing in the sufferings of Christ. Now we need to understand the difference between suffering according to the will of God and suffering because of our ignorance. Many in the body of Christ don't know the difference.

We must comprehend that some things Christ suffered for us as our substitute. And some things Christ suffered for us as our example. To know the difference is to determine whether we walk in victory or defeat. What Christ suffered for us as our substitute we are not to suffer. What are those things? The Word of God teaches us that He became sin so we might be made the righteousness of God in Christ (2 Cor. 5:21).

Therefore we are not to suffer the penalty of sin. He also took our sicknesses as our substitute. Therefore we ought not to suffer sickness and say it is the will of God. Remember the following scripture?

When the even was come, they brought unto him many that were possessed with devils: and he cast out the spirits with his word, and healed all that were sick: that it might be fulfilled which was spoken by Esaias the prophet, saying, Himself took our infirmities, and bare our sicknesses (Matt. 8:16-17).

No, Jesus suffered sickness for us. It is ignorance to say, "I'm suffering this sickness for God's glory." As I said, though, some things Christ suffered as our example. And those were facing tests and trial. Because He suffered being tempted He is able to keep us when we are tempted. He has gone before us to win the victory for us. Notice the following scripture about the temptation of Jesus. "For in that he himself hath suffered being tempted, he is able to succor them that are tempted" (Heb. 2:18). This is what the Word of God means when it talks about the sufferings of Christ.

For as the sufferings of Christ abound in us, so our consolation also aboundeth by Christ. And whether we be afflicted, it is for your consolation and salvation, which is effectual in the enduring of the same sufferings which we also suffer: or whether we be comforted, it is for your consolation and salvation (2 Cor. 1:5-6).

I recall how one of our instructors in Bible school told us that too often we get this business of suffering all mixed up. And certainly that is the case. The Lord will help us in our times of testing, but we ought not to suffer needlessly because of our foolishness or lack of knowledge.

It takes courage to be obedient to the Word of God and the Spirit of God. Can you imagine the courage it took for Abraham to obey the Lord and leave his family and the land he knew so well? Faith and courage are one and the same. Without faith we can have no courage.

One thing we as ministers must understand is that in our walk of obedience if we fail to pass the test we will have to take it again. We will never progress beyond the place where we are now if we fail to be courageous and pass the test in faith. To take the next step demands faith. To make the next move demands faith. But if the Lord has told us to do something He will give us the grace and courage to complete it. Think of it. The Word says:

What shall we then say to these things? If God be for us, who can be against us? He that spared not his own Son, but delivered him up for us all, how shall he not with him also freely give us all things? (Rom. 8:32).

God is for us, so how can we lose? We have been given the name of Jesus! We have been given the armor of God and the gifts of the Spirit.

We have the Word of God and the call of God. We've been given the entire storehouse of heaven—how can we lose? We have the infilling of the Holy Spirit. And we have each other. We have the angels of the Lord who minister to us who are heirs of salvation.

We have been given the blood of Jesus to cleanse us of our sins and the broken body of Jesus to heal our bodies.

How can we lose? We've been given the love of God and the favor of God. How can we lose?

Who shall separate us from the love of Christ? Shall tribulation, or distress, or persecution, or famine, or nakedness, or peril, or sword? (Rom. 8:35).

Nay, in all these things we are more than conquerors through him that loved us. For I am persuaded, that neither death, nor life, nor angels, nor principalities, nor powers, nor things present, nor things to come, Nor height, nor depth, nor any other creature, shall be able to separate us from the love of God, which is in Christ Jesus our Lord (Rom. 8:37-39).

This is why we can take courage and be courageous under fire. Many times, however, what determines whether we are courageous under fire is our attitude. If we look at the pressures of life with the wrong attitude we will fail. Right or wrong thinking can make or break us during times of testing.

If we listen to the devil we will assume that everyone is out to get us. That is one of the devil's biggest lies. If we act on those lies we will run from the battle only to find that the very sword overtakes us we thought we were avoiding. If our minds are not renewed with the Word of God we will not be able to have the courage we need under fire.

COURAGE IN THE FACE OF THE ADVERSARY

The minister must realize that the enemy of our souls will not just sit back and do nothing to stop us. We know people are not our problem in the ministry. The powers of darkness are arrayed against us. They know they don't have long before judgment comes and they are thrown into the bottomless pit forever. So they are working overtime to try to stop the work of God on the earth.

Finally, my brethren, be strong in the Lord, and in the power of his might. Put on the whole armour of God, that ye may be able to stand against the wiles of the devil. For we wrestle not against flesh and blood, but against principalities, against powers, against the rulers of the darkness of this world, against spiritual wickedness in high places (Eph. 6:10-12).

These are the powers that are set against the church. Many of the problems that come against the minister are a direct attack from these powers. But we need to be reminded the Lord has defeated the devil and all his cohorts.

We need to be reminded the devil is under our feet and Jesus defeated him and gave us the victory over him. For without this knowledge the devil will take advantage of our ignorance. If we don't know we have authority over him we will do nothing when the attack comes.

Since we have victory over the devil through the completed work of Jesus on Calvary, we can fear no evil. That's why we have been equipped with the armor of God Paul talks about in the rest of this chapter. Let's look at these verses and notice what God has given to us.

Wherefore take unto you the whole armor of God, that ye may be able to withstand in the evil day, and having done all, to stand. Stand therefore, having your loins girt about with truth, and having on the breastplate of righteousness; and your feet

shod with the preparation of the gospel of peace; above all, taking the shield of faith, wherewith ye shall be able to quench all the fiery darts of the wicked; and take the helmet of salvation, and the sword of the Spirit, which is the word of God: praying always with all prayer and supplication in the Spirit, and watching thereunto with all perseverance and supplication for all saints (Eph. 6:13-18).

So we can observe that we have been given the armor of God. And as ministers we must understand we need this entire armor. Our loins must be dressed with truth. Oh, how we need to understand what this means. Truth here, of course, is the Word of God; but truth here also means we must be honest with others and ourselves.

I dealt with integrity in an earlier chapter, but we should be reminded that as ministers we must be men and women who are not afraid of the truth. Do you remember what Jesus said about this in John 8? Let's take a look.

And ye shall know the truth, and the truth shall make you free. They answered him, We be Abraham's seed, and were never in bondage to any man: how sayest thou, Ye shall be made free? Jesus answered them, Verily, verily, I say unto you, Whosoever committeth sin is the servant of sin (John 8:32-34).

Now the truth Jesus is speaking of here is the Word of God, for He says so. But He refers to another truth here, and that is the truth about oneself. You see, these Jews refused to see the truth about themselves. They were full of pride because they were the physical descendants of Abraham.

Therefore as ministers we must be willing to distinguish the truth about ourselves as we study the Word of God and wait in His presence. Moreover the Holy Spirit will help us grow in all of those areas where we need to change. And all ministers need to change. We must be willing to change, or we will fail to grow and develop the way God wants us to.

To have courage in the face of our adversary we must have the breastplate of righteousness. God has made us His righteousness in Christ. And we need to maintain both the legal and vital sides of righteousness.

For he hath made him to be sin for us, who knew no sin; that we might be made the righteousness of God in him (2 Cor. 5:21).

Without understanding righteousness the minister is at another great disadvantage. But knowing that by the blood of Jesus we are now right with God we can fight the fight of faith and walk in the blessings of the Lord.

We can have courage in the face of the adversary if we walk in the light of the Word and hold up the shield of faith. For the shield of faith will stop all the darts of the enemy. Even as Jesus overcame by the Word of God we likewise overcome by the Word of God.

Then by taking the sword of the Spirit, which is the Word of God, we can go on the offensive. Oh, how we must use our authority! Often ministers fail to remember we have authority over the devil, and as a result we allow him to put us through much unnecessary heartache. We must speak to the devil and command him to stop in all his operations and to desist in all his maneuvers. That's when things will change for us. That's when we need to be reminded we can have the courage sons of God are supposed to have. Therefore stand up and be courageous!

COURAGE IN THE FACE OF
THE WORLD

As ministers we must also have courage in the face of the world. For the world system itself is in opposition to the will of God. Do you remember what the devil tempted Jesus with? He said he would give Jesus all the kingdoms of this world if He would bow down to him.

Again, the devil taketh him up into an exceeding high mountain, and showeth him all the kingdoms of the world, and the glory of them; and saith unto him, All these things will I give thee, if thou wilt fall down and worship me. Then saith Jesus unto him, Get thee hence, Satan: for it is written, Thou shalt worship the Lord thy God, and him only shalt thou serve (Matt. 4:8-10).

The world will place pressure on us to go with them. They are controlled by the devil so the world is against the things of God. But you and I who know the truth know Jesus overcame the world. Because He did we also have overcome the world.

These things I have spoken unto you, that in me ye might have peace. In the world ye shall have tribulation: but be of good cheer; I have overcome the world (John 16:33).

We will have tribulation in this world. But with the boldness of the Holy Spirit and the Word of God we can have courage in the face of the world.

If the world hate you, ye know that it hated me before it hated you. If ye were of the world, the

**world would love his own: but because ye are
not of the world, but I have chosen you out of
the world, therefore the world hateth you (John
15:18-19).**

We recognize that the world hates us, but again we can
rejoice because Jesus has overcome the world and given us
the victory. We can rest in the love of God and have courage
in the face of the world. Persecution will come, but we have
the peace of God.

**Peace I leave with you, my peace I give unto you:
not as the world giveth, give I unto you. Let not
your heart be troubled, neither let it be afraid
(John 14:27).**

**I have given them thy word; and the world hath
hated them, because they are not of the world,
even as I am not of the world. I pray not that thou
shouldest take them out of the world, but that thou
shouldest keep them from the evil. They are not of
the world, even as I am not of the world. Sanctify
them through thy truth: thy word is truth. As
thou hast sent me into the world, even so have I
also sent them into the world (John 17:14-18).**

Therefore as ministers we need not get upset when the
world persecutes us. We must remember that our reward will
be great both in this life and in the life to come. One day our
King will return to this earth, and the whole world will be
made to bow the knee and worship Him. Praise God! What a
wonderful day that will be.

But until that day our joy cannot be taken from us if we
remember what our Lord has done for us in His death, burial
and resurrection. Martin Luther, in his sermon titled "That

a Christian Should Bear His Cross With Patience," makes reference to the following scriptures as he talks about the need for patience:

The Need for It

We must be conformed to the image of the Son of God (Rom. 8:29).

All who desire to live a godly life in Christ Jesus will be persecuted (2 Tim. 3:12).

In the world you have tribulation (John 16:33).

Likewise, "You will be sorrowful; you will weep and lament, but the world will rejoice" (John 16:20).

If we share in [Christ's] sufferings we shall also be glorified with Him (Rom. 8:17).

If you are left without discipline, in which all have participated, then you are illegitimate children and not sons (Heb. 12:8).

Otherwise, what is the purpose of so many comforting passages of Scripture?[21]

One reason I like much of what Martin Luther said is because of the personal study he undertook to come to the conclusion he did. In a time when there was as much persecution in the world as during the time of the early church, Martin Luther realized the value of understanding the Word of God for himself.

Moreover, he was not afraid to speak the truth of the light of the Word of God he had. I believe we as ministers could learn a lot from the commitment these men of God had in yesteryear. Many of them had a lot of courage in the face of the world; they knew the secret that the more the world persecuted them, the more the grace of God sustained them.

Andrew Murray makes the following statements in his sermon "Not of the World":

> **"They are not of the world, even as I am not of the world." That "even as" has a deeper meaning and power than we know. If we suffer the Holy Spirit to unfold that word to us, we shall understand what it is to be in the world as He was in the world. That "even as" has its root and strength in a life union. In it we shall discover the divine secret, that *the more entirely one is not of the world, the more fit he is to be in the world.* The freer the Church is of the spirit and principles of the world, the more influence she will exert in it.**[22]

What a powerful statement! The more we are not of this world, the more fit we are to be in this world. We can have courage in the face of the world, for we are not of this world.

COURAGE IN THE FACE OF
FALSE BRETHREN

Now we come to an area the minister must face if he is not to compromise the Word of God. And that is the persecution that comes from false brethren. The apostle Paul understood this form of persecution. Everywhere he went were those in the church who had wrong motives as so-called ministers.

I believe the persecution from these individuals was the most difficult to bear. I also believe it is this kind of persecution that has hindered the gospel of Jesus Christ more than any other form. Anything other than Christ being the only way to God is religion. As I often say, religion is man's way to God while Christianity is God's way to man.

Religion has sent more people to hell than anything else. This is so because there is a spirit behind religion that comes from the devil. All ministers must comprehend this and know how to resist the pressures of religion that would compromise the truth.

Thrice was I beaten with rods, once was I stoned, thrice I suffered shipwreck, a night and a day I have been in the deep; in journeyings often, in perils of waters, in perils of robbers, in perils by mine own countrymen, in perils by the heathen, in perils in the city, in perils in the wilderness, in perils in the sea, in perils among false brethren (2 Cor. 11:25-27).

Notice that Paul mentions perils among false brethren. When you recognize who you are in Christ, you don't have to fear these false brethren; you just have to proclaim the truth. This is one reason we as ministers must have a good working knowledge of the Word of God. The Greek word that is translated "false" here is a very interesting word. Let's notice the meaning from the Strong's Hebrew Greek Dictionary.

pseudadelphos, psyoo-dad'-el-fos; **from G5571 and G80; a spurious brother, i.e. pretended associate:—false brethren.**

You can see that one meaning of the word "false" here is a "pretended associate." Many in Paul's day wanted to ride his coattail because of his success in ministry. They pretended to be an associate of Paul while at the same time bringing false doctrine. The enemy will do anything to poison the people of God.

And here is where the true minister of the Lord must have courage in the face of these false brethren. I've seen them myself in virtually every place I preach. They are there, and as ministers we need to get a grip on this. If we don't, those who have been planted by the devil will torment us in our churches and in our ministries.

And that because of false brethren unawares brought in, who came in privily to spy out our liberty which we have in Christ Jesus, that they might bring us into bondage: to whom we gave place by subjection, no, not for an hour; that the truth of the gospel might continue with you (Gal. 2:4-5).

We must recognize that the Word of God in its truth will deal with these false brethren. At times the boldness of the Holy Spirit will come upon you to deal with these people, and in those moments you cannot afford to back off. That's when you will need to be courageous in the face of these false brethren.

When the power of the Holy Spirit and the Word of God back you up, you don't have to be afraid of these instruments of the devil. You can walk in the love of God and when needed confront them with that love and the sword of the Spirit, which is the Word of God. Satan's greatest tool has always been to divide and conquer. If he cannot conquer from without, he will try to do so from within.

But as ministers we can have courage in the face of false brethren because greater is He that is in us than he that is in the world. We have the power of God. We have the sword of the Spirit. We have the gifts and manifestations of the Spirit.

One of those gifts is discerning of spirits. We can depend on the greater one in us to expose false brethren.

In 2 Kings 5 we have an example of the power of God revealing to the prophet Elisha the hypocrisy of his servant Gehazi. As a result judgment came upon the servant of Elisha.

And he said unto him, Went not mine heart with thee, when the man turned again from his chariot to meet thee? Is it a time to receive money, and to receive garments, and oliveyards, and vineyards, and sheep, and oxen, and menservants, and maidservants? The leprosy therefore of Naaman shall cleave unto thee, and unto thy seed for ever. And he went out from his presence a leper as white as snow (2 Kings 5:26-27).

God's power has not waned. He is still the all-knowing, all-seeing, all-powerful God of this universe. If we will depend on Him, He will defend us and keep us so that we will not be afraid of false brethren. Our Lord also will give us the courage and boldness to face such individuals. He will give us strength to withstand fear and difficulty. He will give us courage.

---

[18]Ronald F. Youngblood, general editor; F.F. Bruce and R.K. Harrison, consulting editors, *Nelson's new illustrated Bible dictionary: An authoritative one-volume reference work on the Bible with full color illustrations [computer file]*, electronic edition of the revised edition of *Nelson's illustrated Bible dictionary*, Logos Library System, (Nashville: Thomas Nelson) 1997, c1995.

[19]Thomas Nelson Inc., *Heritage of great evangelical teaching: Featuring the best of Martin Luther, John Wesley, Dwight L. Moody, C.H. Spurgeon and others [computer file]*, electronic ed., Logos Library System, (Nashville: Thomas Nelson) 1997, c1996.

[20]Thomas Nelson Inc., *Heritage of great evangelical teaching: Featuring the best of Martin Luther, John Wesley, Dwight L. Moody, C.H. Spurgeon and others [computer file], electronic ed., Logos Library System*, (Nashville: Thomas Nelson) 1997, c1996.

[21]Thomas Nelson Inc., *Heritage of great evangelical teaching: Featuring the best of Martin Luther, John Wesley, Dwight L. Moody, C.H. Spurgeon and others [computer file], electronic ed., Logos Library System*, (Nashville: Thomas Nelson) 1997, c1996.

IV.

DETERMINED TO FINISH THE RACE

Know ye not that they which run in a race run all, but one receiveth the prize? So run, that ye may obtain (1 Cor. 9:24).

Wherefore seeing we also are compassed about with so great a cloud of witnesses, let us lay aside every weight, and the sin which doth so easily beset us, and let us run with patience the race that is set before us (Heb. 12:1).

But none of these things move me, neither count I my life dear unto myself, so that I might finish my course with joy, and the ministry, which I have received of the Lord Jesus, to testify the gospel of the grace of God (Acts 20:24).

Ne of us who have answered the call of God upon our lives to become ministers of the gospel started out one day with the intention of not finishing what the Lord had for us to do. And yet it is sad to realize the number of ministers who for one reason or another have started out running the race with all their hearts only to fall short of the finish line.

I believe you can observe from reading this book there is much more to the ministry than preaching a sermon on Sunday, and so you can also see that thousands of possible reasons exist why some ministers fail. Yet we know the grace of God bestowed upon us was not in vain.

Our Lord didn't call us to start our race and yet not finish it. Indeed it is His will not only that we finish our race but also that we do so with joy. Often it may look as if we are not going to finish it, but in those times an abundance of grace and strength is made real to us so we can move on with God.

All of us have our own race to run. You cannot run my race for me, nor can I run yours for you. We can encourage each other and pray for one another, but it is up to each of us to do the running. Notice what the apostle Paul said in our text. He said first of all that the one running the race must run that he may obtain.

We are not walking blindly without knowing where we are going. No! We are on a path *to* somewhere that we may obtain something. Do you remember what Paul said about obtaining?

Brethren, I count not myself to have apprehended: but this one thing I do, forgetting those things which are behind, and reaching forth unto those things which are before (Phil. 3:13).

Paul understood there were things in front of him to obtain. He chose to forget the past so he could reach for the things before him. You cannot look ahead of and behind you at the same time.

We all have things in our past we wish were different. But we must not focus on the past. The past is over, and we can do nothing about it. Yes, we may learn some lessons from the past, but we cannot live there. Yet I know many ministers are doing just that.

They look at themselves with eyes of contempt and unforgiveness because they have not forgiven themselves over past mistakes. Moreover, many of those mistakes were not their own doing in the first place. Often things happen to the minister that he cannot help, and yet the devil will blame the minister for every aspect of what looks like failure. But the Lord does not see us as a failure. He sees all of us as a success. So we must not look behind us. To finish our race we must be determined to look ahead of us.

Once while in prayer the Lord spoke to me and told me that if only I could see what lay ahead for me I would have cause for much rejoicing. And so it is true for each of us. It doesn't matter your age or how long you've been in the ministry; the Lord has so much more for you than you can see.

That's one reason we walk by faith. For faith is the evidence of things not seen. So we need to run that we may obtain. Obtain the souls and harvest for the Lord. I don't know about you, but I'm not finished yet. I want to see many more won to Jesus before it is too late. I want to see believers obtain all that belongs to them as well.

I want to obtain more of the anointing and refreshing from the Father that I have not yet experienced. I want to walk with the Lord where I've never walked before. I want every day of my life to be an adventure in faith and obedience. I want to recognize that I am not just beating the air as the apostle Paul said.

I want my life to have purpose and meaning, knowing I am in the perfect will of God. It is not enough for me just to finish my race; I want to finish it with joy. As Kenneth Hagin once said in Bible school, "I'd rather set my sights for the stars and reach part of them than to set my sights on nothing and reach all of it."

Does this sound a little bit like you? Do you have the same aspirations? Can you agree with me that it is not enough to finish our race? We must have some souls to sit at Jesus' feet. I believe you feel the same way. But we must all be determined now more than ever before. You see, the temptation to slow down in a race seems to come toward the end of that race. If you are tempted to slow down, realize that now is not the time to do so. You and I are getting closer to the end, and the greatest blessings lie before us.

JESUS OUR EXAMPLE

Jesus saith unto them, My meat is to do the will of him that sent me, and to finish his work (John 4:34).

Looking unto Jesus the author and finisher of our faith; who for the joy that was set before him endured the cross, despising the shame, and is set down at the right hand of the throne of God (Heb. 12:2).

Jesus our Lord is not only our example in life, but He is also our example until the end of life. He is our example in starting our race, and He is our example in finishing our race. And, oh, what an example He has left us to walk in. At any point in His ministry Jesus could have given up. We know this is true because the Word says He was tempted in all points like as we are yet without sin.

For we have not an high priest which cannot be touched with the feeling of our infirmities; but was in all points tempted like as we are, yet without sin (Heb. 4:15).

He could have failed, but He didn't fail. He is our example. He finished His race with joy, and so can you. We can rest in the Lord knowing He will finish in us what He has begun. If Christ is living in you, He will give you the determination to go on in your race and finish it.

We know He cannot fail. We know He understands all that is ahead of us and is already preparing our pathway. We know He will not leave us or abandon us. He has called us to start our race, and He will enable us to finish.

Being confident of this very thing, that he which hath begun a good work in you will perform it until the day of Jesus Christ (Phil. 1:6).

For it is God which worketh in you both to will and to do of his good pleasure (Phil. 2:13).

Now unto him that is able to keep you from falling, and to present you faultless before the presence of his glory with exceeding joy (Jude 24).

Jesus finished His race. And the apostle Paul finished his race. And so can you and I.

We are not of those who give up and quit when the battles come. Remember what the apostle Paul said when he was at the end of his race?

I have fought a good fight, I have finished my course, I have kept the faith (2 Tim. 4:7).

Paul was able to say he had finished his course. How did he do it? Notice that the finishing of his course is sandwiched in between the fact that he fought a good fight and kept the faith.

If we are to finish what the Lord has given us to do on earth, we also must continue to fight a good fight. That means when opposition comes we fight and press through. We must not compromise, but we must *keep* the faith.

In a day when it is so easy to compromise we should remember there are people watching us to see if we will remain true to the faith, including all the biblical doctrines we have learned and have proven in our lives. Keeping the faith means we have been good stewards of that part of the kingdom of God that was committed to us.

It also means we have been true to our own hearts and with honesty and integrity walked in the light of the Word of God. It means being determined not to draw back. For the prize is too great. The reward is too great.

Now the just shall live by faith: but if any man draw back, my soul shall have no pleasure in him. But we are not of them who draw back unto perdition; but of them that believe to the saving of the soul (Heb. 10:38-39).

We are not of those who draw back. Now there are many ways we could draw back. And there are circumstances the enemy could use to try to cause us to draw back. But we have nowhere else to go but forward. And if I were to ask the average minister or layperson if they wanted to draw back they would say, "Of course not."

But for those of us who want nothing less than the perfect will of God we know that simply failing to walk by faith is drawing back—even as the children of Israel drew back the first time they came to the land God wanted them to possess. So it is in the every day issues of life I'm talking about.

At times a minister will face questions and the temptation to quit. You may even ask with your own lips, "What am I doing?" But if the call is there you will never be happy doing anything else. The call of God and the grace of God will sustain you. And with every time you are sustained you will gain confidence. In my own life I have gone the full 360 degrees in my thought process. But I always come back to the fact that I am going to finish all God has for me to do on this earth. In spite of the tests and trials and spiritual attacks something on the inside sustains me. It gives me the courage and the determination to go on.

The rewards and joys that are ahead are too great to turn back. Thank the Lord that if you are called you must be determined to finish the race. I dare to say that one of the lies the devil would throw at us all at one time or another is, "What do think you can do? Can one person really make a difference?" And at those times we must remind ourselves that Jesus thinks so or He would never have called us.

We must encourage ourselves in the Lord and realize God calls those things which are not as though they were. He looks at us and calls us mighty men and women of valor. He is able to see the end from the beginning, and He sees us completing our task. Regardless, the value cannot be placed on a single life of obedience in the kingdom of God. For if only one person is led to the Lord through one life of obedience, then the race is worth it all.

Every minister is valuable. And every ministry is important if it lifts up the cross and the word of faith. Regardless of how small or how large, the importance is equally the same in the plan of God. That's why each of us must be determined to finish our race. Rev. F.B. Meyer, in his sermon "Some Experiences on the Way," gives the following quotation by a Mr. Ruskin.

And Ruskin eloquently forces home on each of us his personal responsibility: "There is work," he says, "for all of us. And there is special work for each, work which I cannot do in a crowd, or as one of a mass, but as one man, acting singly, according to my gifts, and under a sense of my personal responsibilities. I have a special work to do, as one individual, who, by God's plan and appointment, has a separate position, separate responsibilities, and a separate work: a work which, if I do not do it, must be left undone."[23]

And how true it is! We have a work to do. And that work is not done until we have finished our race. As ministers we must be determined to finish our race. Dare we think we have the option of quitting? Dare we think we can give up when our Lord went all the way? Dare we think we can throw away all the blessings waiting for us simply because we may get discouraged in a moment of time?

Determination is something we need more of. According to Webster's New World Dictionary the word "determination" means "a firm intention, the quality of being resolute; firmness of purpose." As ministers of the gospel, oh, how we need a firm intention. We need to be resolute in our purpose. That means not being double minded, but rather being single minded. It means being men and women of purpose and vision.

Yes, determination is something we used to put a greater value on than we do today. People have learned to be fickle. We have made it too easy for them to change their minds. Part of this is attributed to the fast pace of life today. Our culture is so used to having things quickly that patience is a thing of the past. Hence, we live in a generation that changes its mind if things don't work out as quickly as they think it should.

But as ministers we can depend on our Lord to open our eyes to the vision and purpose and value of our calling in Christ Jesus to the extent that nothing but determination is an option. We will then be resolute. We will be unwavering. We will be supercharged with the determination that can only come through the power and anointing of the greater one who lives on the inside of each one of us. We will be filled with His determination to finish in us all He Himself began to do.

---

[23]Thomas Nelson Inc., *Heritage of great evangelical teaching: Featuring the best of Martin Luther, John Wesley, Dwight L. Moody, C.H. Spurgeon and others [computer file], electronic ed., Logos Library System,* (Nashville: Thomas Nelson) 1997, c1996.

XV.

THE JUDGMENT SEAT
OF CHRIST

But why dost thou judge thy brother? or why dost thou set at nought thy brother? for we shall all stand before the judgment seat of Christ. For it is written, As I live, saith the Lord, every knee shall bow to me, and every tongue shall confess to God. So then every one of us shall give account of himself to God (Rom. 14:10-12).

For we must all appear before the judgment seat of Christ; that every one may receive the things done in his body, according to that he hath done, whether it be good or bad (2 Cor. 5:10).

We know from the above scriptures that all of us as believers will appear before the judgment seat of Christ. And as believers we will not have to be afraid of losing our salvation or whether we will live forever in heaven. That was already determined when we gave our hearts to the Lord.

For us who have been born again and made new creatures in Christ the judgment seat of Christ should not be something we dread but something we look forward to with great anticipation. We do not fear eternal damnation because we are washed in the blood of Jesus, but it will also be a sober time; it is then we will either receive our rewards or lose some rewards.

All of us as believers and ministers look forward to that day. In that day we will have our glorified bodies. We will see the one who died for us at Calvary. Our labor will be over. We will have finished our race. And we hope we will be able to say in that day, "Lord, I've completed all You gave me to do on earth."

Let's take some time and discuss the judgments of God, for there is much ignorance of the Word of God in this area. We know that every person on earth will either stand before the judgment seat of Christ if they are born again or stand before God at the great white throne judgment if they have not accepted Christ and be condemned to hell.

And it will be a joy in that day to know we have made the decision here on earth to bow our knees and confess that Jesus is Lord. For those who rejected Christ on the earth it will be a dreadful day. Remember what the Hebrew writer said?

For we know him that hath said, Vengeance belongeth unto me, I will recompense, saith the Lord. And again, The Lord shall judge his people. It is a fearful thing to fall into the hands of the living God (Heb. 10:30-31).

But, as I have said, those of us who have tasted the heavenly gift will have no fear. We will, however, have to give an account of our lives on the earth. If we have obeyed the Lord and walked in His Word and followed His plan for our lives we will be rewarded. If we have failed in areas to obey the Lord we will lose some rewards but we will be saved.

Now if any man build upon this foundation gold, silver, precious stones, wood, hay, stubble; every man's work shall be made manifest: for the day shall declare it, because it shall be revealed by fire; and the fire shall try every man's work of what sort it is. If any man's work abide which he hath built thereupon, he shall receive a reward. If any man's work shall be burned, he shall suffer loss: but he himself shall be saved; yet so as by fire (1 Cor. 3:12-15).

Therefore those of us who are believers must be concerned with whether we build gold, silver and precious stones upon the rock of Jesus Christ. The Believer's Study Bible has some good comments here that would be helpful. Notice the following statements that will shed some light on this subject.

In Rom. 14:10 and 2 Cor. 5:10, this judgment is labeled the *bema* (Gk.) or the "judgment seat" of Christ. Several important truths about that judgment are presented in this passage: (1) only those who have the proper spiritual foundation upon which to construct a life will be able to appear at the *bema*. That foundation is Christ (v. 11). (2) Once the foundation has been laid, believers build a superstructure throughout the years that God allows. That superstructure may consist of the valuable and lasting— gold, silver, precious stones; or the unworthy and fleeting—wood, hay, straw (v. 12). (3) On the day of Christ's return, all works will be declared and "revealed by fire." This latter expression probably refers to the penetrating, purging and discerning gaze of Jesus (cf. Rev. 1:14; 2:18). (4) Those Christian works, which are of permanent value, abide and become the basis for reward (v. 14). (5) Those works which are worthless in them or which are improperly motivated are destroyed in the fire of Christ's gaze. Consequently, reward may be limited, but the man himself is saved (v. 15). This judgment is not to determine salvation or eternal destiny but to determine rewards.[24]

The question remains for us, "Have we obeyed the Lord and run the race He called us to on the earth? Have we walked in the light of the Word of God? Have we judged ourselves when we missed it? Have we laid those sins and mistakes behind us and not picked them up again?

To the one born again this will be the issue of that day. And for us still here on the earth this is the issue today. Oh, thank God for His mercy. Thank Him for the blood of Jesus that has cleansed us from our sins. None of us could dare think of standing before the Lord without the mercy of God and the blood of Jesus upon our lives.

Yes, it is so good to trust in that blood and in the Word of the Lord not only now but in that day. That's the day we work for. That's the day we look forward to. That is part of the prize that is just ahead of us.

IF WE WOULD JUDGE OURSELVES

As believers we have been given the ability by the Lord to judge ourselves. That means that when we miss it and sin we can confess that sin and forgiveness is ours. If we turn from that sin we will not be judged. And when we stand before the Lord that sin will be forgotten because we judged ourselves and were cleansed by the blood of Jesus.

> **For if we would judge ourselves, we should not be judged. But when we are judged, we are chastened of the Lord, that we should not be condemned with the world (1 Cor. 11:31-32).**

> **If we say that we have no sin, we deceive ourselves, and the truth is not in us. If we confess our sins, he is faithful and just to forgive us our sins, and to cleanse us from all unrighteousness (1 John 1:8-9).**

The Lord has given us the power to judge ourselves and confess our sins and receive forgiveness. And here is where many in the body of Christ get confused. Confession is a subject that has been misunderstood over the years. And when one looks at all the scriptures that deal with confession it is easy to understand why.

But for us to understand the doctrine of confession we must do so according to the rules of Bible interpretation. And one of those rules is that we must interpret the Old Testament in the light of the New Testament. If we fail to do so we will get confused. As we study the New Testament we find six kinds of confession.

Each one of these confessions has a different purpose. If we are not careful we could mix them up and fail to walk in the light of the Word of God in this area. I feel it is necessary to bring some clarification on the subject here.

CONFESSION OF SINS UNDER THE MINISTRY OF JOHN THE BAPTIST

The first kind of confession we find in the New Testament is the confession of sins under the ministry of John the

Baptist. Now this confession of sins by the lost was the same confession we had in the Old Testament. Notice the following scripture:

> **I acknowledged my sin unto thee, and mine iniquity have I not hid. I said, I will confess my transgressions unto the Lord; and thou forgavest the iniquity of my sin (Ps. 32:5).**

Jesus had not yet come and made redemption for our sins. Therefore the confession of sin under the Old Testament period was to receive forgiveness for sins but not remission of sins. In the Old Testament the saints who trusted God for their salvation by faith looked *forward* to the coming of the Christ who would then remit or take away their sins.

But now that Christ has come and brought redemption through His blood, we look *back* to the cross and have faith in the completed work of Christ. In the Old Testament no one was born again. But in the New Testament we have been born again. Therefore when the people came to be baptized by John they confessed their sins looking forward to the coming Messiah.

> **And there went out unto him all the land of Judaea, and they of Jerusalem, and were all baptized of him in the river of Jordan, confessing their sins (Mark 1:5).**

The next confession we have in the New Testament is the confession of Jesus as Lord in order to be born again. Now this is where many have misunderstood the scripture. Today the sinner does not confess his or her sins to be born again or saved.

Today the sinner confesses Jesus as Lord. This of course is the most important confession we could ever make. Please notice the following scripture.

That if thou shalt confess with thy mouth the Lord Jesus, and shalt believe in thine heart that God hath raised him from the dead, thou shalt be saved. For with the heart man believeth unto righteousness; and with the mouth confession is made unto salvation (Rom. 10:9-10).

Whosoever shall confess that Jesus is the Son of God, God dwelleth in him, and he in God (1 John 4:15).

So we can see from these verses that it is the confession of the Lordship of Jesus that determines if one is saved or not. And let me say that this confession must come from a heart that is sincere. Now the third confession is the confession of the believer of his sins when he is out of fellowship with the Lord. When the believer sins fellowship is broken between that believer and the Lord, but when that believer confesses that sin fellowship is restored.

If we say that we have no sin, we deceive ourselves, and the truth is not in us. If we confess our sins, he is faithful and just to forgive us our sins, and to cleanse us from all unrighteousness (1 John 1:8-9).

The confession of the believer of sin is not to be confused with the confession of the sinner who is saved by confessing the Lordship of Jesus. Finally there is the confession of the believer of who we are in Christ. This is the confession the Word of God says about us as believers. This of course is the positive side of the subject of confession. Few Christians know about this kind of confession. It seems the only side of confession that most are familiar with is the negative side, which is the confessing of sins.

Since then we have a great high priest who has passed through the heavens, Jesus the Son of God, let us hold fast our confession. For we do not have a high priest who cannot sympathize with our weaknesses, but One who has been tempted in all things as we are, yet without sin (Heb. 4:14-15, NASB).

The fifth kind of confession in the New Testament is the confession of our faults one to another. This kind of confession is found in the book of James.

Confess your faults one to another, and pray one for another, that ye may be healed. The effectual fervent prayer of a righteous man availeth much (James 5:16).

Now this is not talking about trying to dream up some mistake and telling it to the church. This is talking about being real with one another when in need. It's talking about having the church stand with you when you need help in overcoming in an area.

Then we come to the sixth and last confession we find in the New Testament. And this is a very sad one. For it is the confession that Jesus is the Son of God by the lost on the judgment day. On that day everyone who refused to confess the Lordship of Jesus on earth will bow before God and confess that Jesus is Lord. Only it will be too late on that day.

Wherefore God also hath highly exalted him, and given him a name which is above every name:

That at the name of Jesus every knee should bow, of things in heaven, and things in earth, and things under the earth; and that every tongue should confess that Jesus Christ is Lord, to the glory of God the Father (Phil. 2:9-11).

So when we stand before the judgment seat of Christ we will be glad we were not ashamed to confess His name before men while we were still on the earth. For the minister of the gospel who has obeyed the Lord it will be a glorious time.

I can't think of a better motivator to encourage us to do what the Lord wants us to do than to realize we have only one life here on earth and one opportunity to achieve the destiny that awaits us. On that day may all of us hear Him say, "Well done, thou good and faithful servant" (Matt. 25:21).

Eternity is a very long time compared to this life. Indeed all our years put together cannot compare to eternity. What is one hundred years compared to eternity? What is a thousand years compared to eternity? Our minds cannot even grasp it.

I'm convinced it will take all of eternity to learn of the absolute glory and brightness of the person of our Father God and Lord Jesus Christ. We can't even conceive of what it will be like with a glorified body! To have a body like His glorious body, without pain and death able to touch it, is nearly beyond words.

I believe it would do us all some good just to think of the glories that are awaiting us on the other side. Yes, to think of the streets of gold and the gates of pearl. To think of our loved ones we will see again and the fact that the very atmosphere is supercharged with the light of God.

I believe we are so much closer to that day than we can imagine. Yes, eternity is just a breath away. It is a blink of an eye away. All of us should be ready for that day; but those of us who are ministers of the gospel would do well to stay ready so we will fulfill all the good pleasure of His will.

I don't know about you, but I sense a growing anticipation and longing for that day in my heart. With each passing day and week and month I look forward more and more to the glories that await us on the other side.

---

[24]W.A. Criswell, *Believer's study Bible [computer file], electronic ed.*, *Logos Library System*, (Nashville: Thomas Nelson) 1997, c1991 by the Criswell Center for Biblical Studies.

[22]Thomas Nelson Inc., *Heritage of great evangelical teaching: Featuring the best of Martin Luther, John Wesley, Dwight L. Moody, C.H. Spurgeon and others [computer file], electronic ed.*, *Logos Library System*, (Nashville: Thomas Nelson) 1997, c1996.

CONCLUSION

Within the pages of this book are some things that comprise the minister's life of obedience. But it is a life that is both challenging and rich with rewards. It is a life of service that begins with the highest calling in the universe, the call of God. It is a life of progress and learning on a continual basis, a life that never stops developing. From the calling to the separation by the Holy Spirit and on to the qualifying by the Holy Spirit, it is an ever-upward climb.

We've learned that to be a minister who brings glory to the Lord, the life of the Lord must live in and through him. The minister's life is one of faith where we become all things to all men through the love of God in us, and where one is as valuable as hundreds or even thousands.

The minister's life of obedience is one of service. We must strive to maintain that servant's heart of compassion and refuse to allow the things of this world to harden our hearts and cause the ministry to become only an occupation. It is a life that sees the best in every person even as Christ sees the best in us.

The minister's life must be one of integrity and honesty. Our lives cannot be compromised by this world where the lust of other things would blind us to the one thing that should mean the most to us, our integrity. The servant of the Lord must walk against the flow of the world, which is controlled by the powers of darkness.

Without being willing to be persecuted for the gospel's sake, the minister will not be able to say to those who need Jesus and to the church, "Follow me as I follow Christ." We've learned that the minister's life should reflect the Lord Jesus in every aspect so that with purpose his or her life will become a light in this world.

We have learned that for the minister to maintain the joy of the Lord and the fulfillment of his call he or she must press into the things of God as a way of life. With the passing of every single day there must be in the heart of the minister a faith in the plan of God that waits the day. By pressing toward the mark of the high calling of God his life is always one of change and blessing.

The minister's life of obedience is one of learning to rest in the anointing and the power of the Holy Spirit who has sealed him. The minister must come to the knowledge of understanding the sphere of influence that has been granted by God. And by working in that sphere where the Lord has placed him the minister will grow in the appreciation of the people who surround his life.

One vital aspect of the minister's life is that of courage in the face of adversity. Equipped by the Word of God and the anointing there should grow with each passing year a determination to finish the race the Lord has assigned to him.

So much more comprises the life of the minister, and only a few of the essentials are stated here. These are some of the most important essentials I believe many times are left untold.

To all who read this book my prayer is that you have been challenged and inspired to fulfill your destiny. And I trust this book has stirred within you a greater determination in your own life to ask yourself, "Am I living the minister's life of obedience?"

BIBLIOGRAPHY

Baxter, Richard. *The Reformed Pastor.* Portland, Oregon: Multnomah Press, 1982.

Copeland, Kenneth. *Walking in Honesty, Truth and Integrity.* Tulsa, Oklahoma: Harrison House, 1994.

Criswell, W.A. *Believer's Study Bible.* Nashville, TN: [computer file] electronic ed. Logos Library System, 1997, c 1996.

Hagin, Kenneth E. *How You Can Be Led by the Spirit of God.* Tulsa, Oklahoma: Faith Library Publications, 1986.

Maxwell, John. *People Power: Life's Little Lessons on Relationships.* Tulsa, Oklahoma: Honor Books Inc., 1996.

McGee, Vernon. *Thru the Bible Commentary.* Nashville, TN: [computer file] electronic ed. Logos Library System, 1997, c 1996.

Nelson, Thomas. *Heritage of Great Evangelical Teaching:* Featuring the best of Martin Luther, John Wesley, Dwight L. Moody, C.H. Spurgeon and others [computer file] electronic ed. Logos Library System, 1997, c 1996.

Nelson, Thomas. *King James Version Study Bible*. Nashville, TN: |computer file| electronic ed. Logos Library System, 1995-97.

Nelson, Thomas. *New American Standard Bible*. Nashville, TN: The Lockman Foundation, 1977.

Nelson, Thomas. *New Revised Standard Version*. Nashville, TN: Division of Christian Education of the National Council of the Church of Christ, c 1989.

Simon & Schuster, *Webster's New World Dictionary*. New York, NY. Paramount Communications Company, 1994.

Strong, James, *New Exhaustive Concordance of the Bible*. Nashville, TN: Thomas Nelson Publishers, 1990.

The Amplified Bible, Expanded Edition. Grand Rapids, Michigan: Zondervan Publishing House, 1965.

Vine, W.E., Merrill F. Unger and William White. *Vine's Complete Expository Dictionary of Old and New Testament Words*. Nashville, TN: |computer file| electronic ed. Logos Library System, 1997, c 1996.

Wilkinson, Bruce, and Kenneth Boa. *Talk Thru the Bible*. Nashville, TN: |computer file| electronic ed. Logos Library System, 1997, c 1996.

Young, Robert. *Young's Literal Translation of the Bible*. Grand Rapids, Michigan: Guardian Press.

Youngblood, Ronald F., F.F. Bruce and R.K. Harrison. *Nelson's New Illustrated Bible Dictionary*. Nashville, TN: |computer file| electronic ed. Logos Library System, 1997, c 1996.

LaVergne, TN USA
21 October 2009
161648LV00001B/9/A